GOD DELIGHTS IN YOU

GOD DELIGHTS IN YOU

An Introduction to Gospel Spirituality

JOHN T. CATOIR, J.C.D.
Director of the Christophers

The ❦ Christophers
12 East 48th Street, New York, NY 10017

Library of Congress Cataloging-in-Publication Data

Catoir, John T.
    God delights in you: an introduction to Gospel spirituality / John T. Catoir.
        p.   cm.
    ISBN: 0-8189-0594-8
    1. God — Love. 2. Spiritual life — Catholic authors. I. Title.
BT140.C295   1990
248—dc20
                                          90-41425
                                            CIP

Designed, printed and bound in the United States of America by the Fathers and Brothers of the Society of St. Paul, 2187 Victory Boulevard, Staten Island, New York 10314, as part of their communications apostolate.

Printing Information:

Current Printing - first digit 1 2 3 4 5 6 7 8 9 10 11 12

Year of Current Printing - first year shown
1990   1991   1992   1993   1994   1995   1996   1997

For those who defy Him
God's love is a sorrowing love,
For those who stumble
God's love is a merciful love,
For those who strive to love Him
God's love is a joyful love.

This book is dedicated to
everyone who wants to love God,
Particularly to my brother priests,
who delight the Lord more than they know.

TABLE OF CONTENTS

"I was abandoned to a thousand thoughts, and for many days, had attempted mightily to discover myself and what was good for me, and what evil to avoid, when suddenly — was it myself or was it another, I do not know, and that was precisely what I ardently sought to know. Anyway, it was said to me, 'If you find what you seek, what will you do with it? Who will you entrust it to before you die?'

"I answered, 'I will keep it in my memory.'

"But can your memory keep everything your mind has perceived? Indeed, it cannot. You must write, then . . . ask for strength so that you may find what you seek: then write it down, so that this child-bearing of your heart may quicken it and make it strong. Write only the results, and spare the words. Think not of the many that may read these pages, a few will understand.'"

St. Augustine
(Opening Lines of "The Soliloquy")

INTRODUCTION

Everything that emanates from God's life is personal. His love for you is not an abstract religious truth. It is a power that flows from the depths of His personal life.

In the Sermon on the Mount (Mt 5:3-12), Jesus preached the Good News. He said, *Blessed are the poor in spirit* . . . This means that you are highly favored by God when you are childlike in spirit. I have adapted the Beatitudes slightly to put them in a language that is more personal.

You delight me when you are poor in spirit,
You delight me when you are meek and humble of heart,
You delight me when you long to be just and good,
You delight me when you are kind and merciful,
You delight me when you are pure of heart,
You delight me when you strive for peace,
You delight me when you suffer on my account . . .
Rejoice and be glad, for I am preparing
a fantastic reward
for you.

Jesus taught us that God's hidden face is full of tender compassion. The people of ancient times generally thought of God as a jealous, vengeful judge, but Jesus brought us a different message. He taught us that God wants to heal and save us because we are His children. We belong to Him. This revelation is not given as a theological concept, but as a comforting reality in the here and now. The Gospel is indeed good news.

Some may find it difficult to imagine God delighting in His creation. They are understandably troubled by the presence of evil in the world. Malicious individuals like Hitler and Stalin have poisoned the atmosphere in this century so that one can more easily imagine God being angry rather than delighted. And yet, the Scriptures tell us of God's delight: *You shall be called, 'My delight'... for the Lord delights in you and will claim you as His own* (Is 62:4).

The history of salvation began when God claimed the people of Israel as His own: *For the Lord takes delight in His people* (Ps 149).

Faith in God's saving love is not a fantasy trip. It is certain knowledge revealed to us in the Bible. We may not always understand the mystery behind the facts, but this we know: God's love is personal. He made a personal commitment to us, and Jesus has assured us of the Father's abiding love.

Some of us are better than others at responding to God's love. There are times when we have not been as pleasing to God as we would like, but the saints were not saintly every minute of the day either.

The Lord challenges us to take up our cross and follow Him, but He does this with a gentle touch. Remember those words of Jesus to the woman taken in adultery: *Has no one condemned you? Then neither do I condemn you. Go and sin no more* (Jn 8:10, 11). God overlooks much and forgives all in the lives of those who seek His mercy.

He wants us to be His disciples: *If you insist on saving your life, you will lose it. Only those who throw away their lives for my sake and for the sake of the Good News will ever know what it means to really live* (Mk 8:35).

God wants us to be good, but His love does not depend upon our goodness. Divine love is unchanging. It never recedes or lessens because of our unworthiness. Love is not one of His *attributes*; it is His very *essence*.

This amazing truth is both fascinating and understandable. Jesus assured us in the parable of the Prodigal Son that the Father never stops loving us even when we stray. The Old Testament was not always so optimistic about God's mercy. In the book of Sirach, for example, we read: *Say not "Great is his mercy; my many sins he will forgive."* . . . *At the time of vengeance, you will be destroyed* (Si 5:6, 9).

Jesus opposed this concept and was condemned for teaching that God's mercy extended even to the apostate and the sinner: *Indeed, God did not send the Son into the world to condemn the world, but in order that the world might be saved through Him* (Jn 3:17). In fact, *God so loved the world that He gave His only Son, so that everyone who believes in Him may not perish but may have eternal life* (Jn 3:16).

As a Catholic priest, I claim no special charism for teaching religion, but I have made some personal discoveries along the way. In the study of Scripture, there are times when a truth you have known all your life suddenly hits you in a new way. This happened to me when I thought more about the meaning of God's love. A lover delights in being with his beloved. Isn't that true? What happens if you apply that simple idea to God and you? It means that God delights in loving you.

As I progressed in the knowledge of God's love, I began to sense His delight more and more. I became happier, more joyful, more at peace with myself. In small ways my life began to change for the better. As I reflected on what was happening to me, I realized that a major shift had taken place in my thinking. I was beginning to live my life in a different way. I had always focused on avoiding sin, eradicating evil inclinations, overcoming temptation. But now I began to frame a more positive spirituality. While still trying to avoid sin, I put more emphasis on trying to please God instead of merely striving not to displease Him. This shift opened my soul to a new spirit of freedom and joy.

I began to visualize God's delight with my efforts. And so resisting a temptation was now a joy because I knew it pleased the Lord when I succeeded. Unfortunately I didn't always succeed. Nevertheless, I knew God was pleased with my efforts. I began to think of myself as a saint-in-training, rather than a miserable sinner. My hope in God's strength became more alive, and I was less fearful about incurring His wrath.

When a child is learning to walk, does the parent become angry if he flops every now and then? Of course not. If you think about it from God's perspective, the doctrine of divine love is wonderfully reassuring. God loves all His children. They are all made in His image and likeness, and He delights in each one of them. We should all rejoice in that knowledge, and live in that light.

"The just will rejoice, not in the world, but in the Lord. Light has dawned for the just . . . Love, and He will draw near; love, and He will dwell within you. The Lord is at hand; have no anxiety" (St. Augustine).

As a mother delights in her infant child, so does the Lord delight in us. Rosa Blanes from Edmonton, Canada wrote to me recently about the joys of motherhood. She said that even though a baby can be messy and demanding at times, a mother doesn't really care. She cleans up her little one and carries on. Mrs. Blanes put it this way, "Nuzzling a bathed, powdered, sweet sleepy baby is a delight. God must be delighted with His children in a similar way."

God's love is infinitely greater than the noblest human love. We are not sweet smelling babies, yet His love enfolds us in wondrous ways. How much easier it is for us to love the Lord when we realize that He is disposed to delight in us, individually and personally.

Some of us were raised to think of God as easily offended and quick to punish. Isn't it time we started to take Him at His word? *As the Father has loved me, so I have loved you* (Jn 15:9). "To be" is to be loved. We were created out of love. Our union with God begins at conception and is intensified by the Sacrament of Baptism, which makes us children of God in a special way.

God's plan for us is only beginning to unfold. We have an eternity to explore the meaning of His love. But this much we know right now: our holiness is a gift from God.

— Holiness is not something we earn by being good;
  we are good because we are holy.
— Holiness is not a reward for avoiding evil;
  we avoid evil because we are holy.
— Holiness is not the fruit of a prayerful life;
  we pray because we are holy.
— Holiness is not bestowed on us after a lifetime of service;
  we give a lifetime of service because we are holy.

Even though holiness is a gift, it is a gift that increases in proportion to our openness and willingness to grow spiritually. This is accomplished through a lifelong process involving love and sacrifice. Some of us are holier than others, closer to God, more perfectly conformed to His will. Each person is unique, and each relationship with God is unique, and so comparisons are unwise. We do need, though, to look more closely at the way we grow in holiness.

We know that grace builds on nature. What is this nature we speak of? Aren't some of us gifted with a rich nature while others are deprived from birth? Some have a high I.Q., others do not. There seems to be an unfair distribution of natural gifts and talents. If openness is all we need, some will do better than others. A small cup is not the same as a five-gallon jar. But, unlike the cup which is forever a puny little cup, we are capable of expansion and growth.

Suppose you are going to fill some container and you know you will be given a large amount. Then you set about stretching your sack or wineskin or whatever it is. Why? Because you know the quantity you will have to put in it and your eyes tell you there is not enough room. By stretching it, therefore, you increase the capacity of the sack, and this is how God deals with us. Simply by making us wait, He increases our desire, which in turn enlarges the capacity of our soul, making it able to receive what is to be given. So, my brethren, let us continue to desire, for we shall be filled.

(St. Augustine, *Commentary on 1 John*)

No matter what your limitations might be, God delights in helping you to grow in your capacity for greater happiness. If only by waiting and hoping and longing, we are expanding the soul's capacity for holiness and happiness. When you cooperate with God, your progress is even more rapid. It delights Him to see you grow up spiritually. He wants your happiness, and He will help you every step of the way.

What does it mean to delight the Lord?

Delight is pleasure at high tide. God delights in loving you, especially when you respond to His graces. His love does not depend on your faith, or your hope, or, for that matter, your love of Him. His love is ever-flowing, like the rays of the sun. However, your happiness does depend on your own desires. If they are selfish, you will sink into misery. Jesus told us to obey His supreme commandment of love. In doing that, we will abide in His joy. Everything that is selfish leads to narrowness and grief. So the grand plan is clear. Pray for the grace to understand it and live by it. Ask, and you will receive happiness in abundance.

If you have faith, you know your Maker is close to you throughout all the storms of life. He is there supporting you when you labor in a mist of confusion. He is there giving you clarity and comfort when you turn to Him for support. The saints knew this tension, and they coped as best they could: *Forgetting the past, and looking forward to what lies ahead, I strain to reach the end of the race and receive the prize for which God is calling us up to heaven because of what Christ Jesus did for us* (Ph 3:13, 14).

Most of us know the truths of revelation, but we forget to apply them to daily life. This book is written to help you to stir up the faith that is already in you. Read it in small bites. And if you come across a line that stirs your heart, rest a moment in that love.

You may find the material repetitious. I have been deliberately repetitious because great truths need to be repeated until they are deeply believed. Try not to let your doubts take over. I am fully aware that the Lord said, *Take up your cross and follow me,* and that God cannot be reduced to a country gentleman who makes no demands on us. But I believe we are called, above all, to open ourselves to His love. This is the challenge of Christianity. Jesus taught us this great lesson on the cross: accepting the life God has destined for us, and living it as courageously as possible, is the highest act of worship we can offer to the Father.

Carrying the cross is so much easier when you sense God smiling down upon you. He wants to give you comfort and relief for all eternity. In the bright promise of the resurrection, may you feel the power of the Risen Lord working miracles in your life. May your faith be strong and unwavering, and may you love God, not so much for what He can do for you, but for Himself alone. The Lord is personally aware of every movement of your heart, and He takes enormous delight in your efforts to love Him well.

I want to thank my editor, Joseph Thomas, and those who have made suggestions along the way to improve the manuscript: José and Catherine de Vinck, Dolores Ammar, Marie Leyhan, Ann Nunziato, Margaret O'Connell, Helen LeGrande, Mrs. Charles Widmann and Monsignor John Demkovich. Their help has been invaluable.

I hope you enjoy this little book. I offer it with much love.

Father John Catoir
Easter, 1990

GOD DELIGHTS IN YOU

In my syndicated column I asked my readers to share their thoughts on God's delight. I received hundreds of wonderful replies confirming my feeling that most Catholics enjoy the idea that God really does love them.

I am deeply grateful to everyone who wrote to share a special thought with me. Some preferred that I not use their name, or that I use only their initials. I am respecting their wishes. Because of a limitation of space, I could not print every letter, but I am most appreciative to all those who took the time to share their personal reflections.

(From Bruce Snowden, Bronx, NY)

That I could delight Almighty God, the Awesome, Holy One, the Creator of all that is seen and unseen, even once *would be enough to keep me happy all life long! The very thought that such a thing is possible destroys anxiety and withers away depression. How I wish this mood would persist, day in and day out, never ending. But alas, being made of flesh and blood, and of vacillating spirit, the joy of knowing that God delights in me often grows dim. I am ever in need of spiritual recharging.*

Quite literally, I can think of a thousand ways God delights in me: God delights in me when I accept the material limitations resulting from our decision (my wife's and mine) to send our children through Catholic schools, when a public school education would put thousands of dollars in saved tuition into our pockets, allowing that annual vacation others always seem to take. God delights in me, when, for example, my Pastor needs help on some parish project and I volunteer to give a hand again. He delights in me when local kids need a basketball court refurbished and I make it happen. God delights in me when, on my way to work on the subway, a derelict asks me for the cup of coffee I am drinking, and I give it to him. I know God delights in me when I enjoy the bounty of His material goodness, such as a fine meal my wife prepares for me or that delicious spinach and okra soup with cornmeal dumplings that Mom sometimes makes. God delights in me when I try to follow the teachings of the Catholic Church (often with difficulty but with firm resolve) as I seek to emulate Jesus and the Christian commitment of the saints. Yes I am firmly convinced that God delights in me despite the fact that "I am with great ease a pagan, and with great difficulty a Christian!"

CHAPTER ONE

Jesus Brings Good News

There are two images of God presented in the Bible. The Hebrew Bible often depicts Him as mean and punishing if you disobey Him; the New Testament emphasizes the fact that He is a loving, caring God. In some of the Psalms, for example, sinners are cursed. Only those who remain faithful to Yahweh can count on His protection: *Lay your scourge aside. I am worn out with the blows you deal me. You punish man with the penalties of sin, like a moth you eat away at all that gives him pleasure* (Ps 39). In the New Testament, Jesus presents Yahweh as a God who sees His children as precious: *Are not two sparrows sold for a penny? Yet not one of them will fall to the ground without your Father's willing it . . . Fear not, therefore; you are of more value than many sparrows* (Mt 10:29-30).

The Scriptures were written over a period of thousands of years. We have only been able to assimilate God's unfolding revelation a little at a time. As a result there are sections of the Hebrew Bible that do not seem to be in harmony with other parts of Scripture. For instance, the Torah (which comprises the first five books of the Old Testament) never mentions the word "resurrection." Consequently, the Sadducees who were the biblical literalists of Jesus' time, refused to believe in an afterlife. The Pharisees, on the other hand, did believe in the resurrection, based on a freer interpretation of the Scriptures.

3

Jesus, of course, taught us to hope for a place in the Kingdom of Heaven: *If anyone believes in me, even though he dies, will live; he will never die* (Jn 11:26).

In one section of the Torah, God curses the disobedient (cf. Dt 27), but in the Book of Exodus we read that Yahweh is *a God tender and actively favoring His loved one, slow to anger and rich in loyal attachment*. This is no contradiction. Yahweh and the Jewish law form one entity. Anyone who violates the law turns away from God Himself. The greatest sin of all was to deny one's Jewishness. Such an act severed one from membership in God's family and incurred His wrath. Orthodox Jews always considered apostasy to be the greatest depravity. Consequently, while the covenant-God in the Hebrew Bible is often described as tender, loyal and affirming of His people, He remains so only so long as they are His loyal and obedient subjects.

Jesus came with a profoundly more nuanced interpretation of the Bible. He described God's attitude toward the sinner in this way: *God so loved the world that He gave His only Son so that* everyone *who believes in Him may not be lost but have eternal life* (Jn 3:16). It was revolutionary to say that God loves *everyone* in the world, for that would include sinners and even apostates. Jesus told the parable of the prodigal son where the father forgives the son and throws a party for him when he returns from his wild living. Here, Jesus was going directly against the teachings of the Book of Deuteronomy where we read: *If a man has a stubborn and rebellious son who will not listen to the voice of his father and mother . . . they shall report him to the elders of his town where they will say: "This son of ours is a wastrel and a drunkard." Then all his fellow citizens shall stone him to death. You must banish this evil from your midst* (21:18-21).

Jesus knew He was facing the death penalty if He persisted in challenging the Torah the way He did. It was

written: *If a prophet or a dreamer of dreams arises among you
and offers to do a sign or a wonder for you . . . do not listen to his
words . . . that prophet or dreamer of dreams must be put to
death, for he preached apostasy from Yahweh* (Dt 13:2-3). Any
deviation from the strict punishments proposed by the law was
thought to be a violation of the covenant and a betrayal of
Yahweh.

Jesus did not back off though. His amazing courage is
rarely understood. It was His mission to liberate His people
from the oppression of the law. St. Paul is among the first fruits
of His teachings: . . . *no one can be justified in the sight of God
by keeping the law* (Rm 3:20). Needless to say, this is quite a
departure from the ancient teachings.

The Pharisees generally saw Jesus as a false and danger-
ous prophet. His attack on orthodoxy could not be tolerated
without risking the displeasure of Yahweh Himself, for the law
is clear concerning false prophets: *You must not listen to him,
you must show him no pity, you must not spare him, you must
not conceal his guilt. No, you must kill him* (Dt 13:9). The
Bible demanded punishment in no uncertain terms. It was
idolatry to distort the law: *You must add nothing to what I
command and take nothing from it* (Dt 4:2).

There are many such examples where Jesus boldly challenged the Torah. In the matter of warfare, for instance, the
Hebrew Bible teaches that despised enemies of Israel were to
be destroyed or punished severely. Jesus said, *You have
learned how it was said in the past, "An eye for an eye and a
tooth for a tooth." But I say to you: offer the wicked man no
resistance. On the contrary, if anyone hits you on the right
cheek, offer him the other as well* (Mt 5:38). This was ridiculous
to His contemporaries. Even in our own day, in so-called
Christian nations, this level of virtue is not practiced. One can
only imagine how the Jews of old must have reacted to it.

On another point, the Torah demanded that the people of

Israel treat one another righteously. Isaiah (58:5-8) gives us some insight into this noble ideal. In this text God is lamenting the fact that His people are more concerned with rituals than with true charity:

> *Is that the sort of fast that pleases me,*
> *a truly penitential day for men?*
> *Hanging your head like a reed,*
> *lying down on sackcloth and ashes?*
> *Is this what you call fasting,*
> *a day acceptable to Yahweh?*
> *Is not this the sort of fast that pleases me*
> *— it is the Lord Yahweh who speaks —*
> *to break unjust fetters*
> *and undo the thongs of the yoke,*
> *to let the oppressed go free,*
> *and break every yoke,*
> *to share your bread with the hungry,*
> *and shelter the homeless poor,*
> *to clothe the man you see naked,*
> *and not to turn from your own kin?*
> *Then will the light shine like the dawn*
> *and your wound be quickly healed over.*

There is a strong sense of love conveyed here. Love is the motivating force behind all righteousness. However God's love is reserved for the good people of Israel: *If you do not obey the voice of Yahweh your God, nor keep and observe all the commandments and statutes of His that I enjoin on you today, then all the curses that follow shall come upon you and overtake you* (Dt 28:15). Those who had apostatized from their Jewish faith, or disobeyed it, thus becoming defiled, fell into the hands of the priests who either punished them or required that they perform some special ritual purifications.

It is clear that the Old Testament is not the New. Jesus

stood against a mighty tradition that had been handed down from Moses. He never attacked Moses himself but He challenged the way Moses was interpreted. When Jesus condemned divorce (Mt 19:1-12), His critics said, *"Why then did Moses command that a writ of dismissal should be given in the case of divorce?"* Jesus replied, *"It was because you were so unteachable that Moses allowed you to divorce your wives, but it was not like this from the beginning."* Jesus is telling them that the Mosaic Law has been corrupted. In another section, however, he insists, *Do not imagine that I have come to abolish the Law or the Prophets. I have come not to abolish but to complete them. I tell you solemnly till heaven and earth disappear, not one dot, not even one stroke, shall disappear from the law until its purpose is achieved* (Mt 5:17).

Jesus claimed He was teaching a new ethical standard, higher than the old, but not essentially different from it: *You have learned how it was said to our ancestors: "You must not commit adultery." But I say this to you: if a man looks at a woman lustfully, he has already committed adultery with her in his heart. If your right eye should cause you to sin, tear it out and throw it away; for it will do you less harm to lose one part of you than to have your whole body go to hell* (Mt 5:27-31).

Jesus referred to Himself as the Son of God, and He performed miracles: healing the sick, raising the dead, pardoning sins, challenging and modifying sacred laws. He did these things not the way the prophets of old did them, as reluctant agents — the prophets were rarely volunteers — but rather He acted in His own name, claiming that all authority had been given to Him by His Father.

And you'll notice that Jesus never called God, "Yahweh," except when quoting from the Bible itself. He preferred to call Him, "Father." In Matthew (11:27) and Mark (14:36), He addressed God using the Aramaic word, "Abba," or as a child would say, "Daddy." This was a form of filial affection that Jesus encouraged His followers to use when addressing God.

He never used the term "Father" in a universal sense, the way one might call God the Father of Israel. His use of the word "Father" expressed the unique relationship of a father and a son. *Yes, Father, for such was Your good pleasure. All things have been delivered to Me by My Father, and no one knows the Son except the Father, nor does anyone know the Father except the Son, and him to whom the Son chooses to reveal Him* (Mt 11:25-27).

The key difference between the New and the Old Testaments is, of course, Jesus Christ. He is the fullness of the Father's revelation. As such, He is central to the divine plan of salvation. Jesus is the privileged channel of communication with God. He is the Mediator of God's love. He established a Church to bring the Good News of salvation to all the world: *Go, therefore; make disciples of all the nations, baptizing them in the name of the Father, and of the Son, and of the Holy Spirit. Teach them to observe all the commands I gave you* (Mt 28:19).

Jesus taught that God is love. The Father's love is universal, like the rain falling on everyone, the good and the bad alike. He insisted that His followers should love one another in the same way.

In the Acts of the Apostles (10:34-36, 43), St. Peter, fresh from the memory of Jesus, had this interesting insight: *The truth I have now come to realize is that God does not have favorites, but that anybody of any nationality who fears God and does what is right is acceptable to Him. It is true, God sent His Word to the people of Israel and it was to them that the good news of peace was brought by Jesus Christ — but Jesus Christ is the Lord of all . . . it is to Him that all the prophets bear witness that all who believe in Jesus will have their sins forgiven through His name.* Jesus taught us to love one another even to the point of folly: *Everyone who hears these words of mine and acts on them is like a wise man who built his house on rock; and the rain fell, and the torrents came, and the winds blew and battered that house, but it did not fall, because it was founded on rock* (Mt 7:24-25).

Those who take Christ's words to heart will come to the knowledge of the truth and be saved. *I have come like a light into the world* (Jn 12:46). Once we receive His light, we in turn are to become a light for others: *You are like a city on a hill, glowing in the night for all to see . . . Do not hide your light! Let it shine for all to see. Let your good deeds glow for all to see so that they will praise your Father in heaven* (Mt 5:14-16).

While the New Testament is not the Old, we do celebrate certain truths in common. A special benediction in the Book of Deuteronomy speaks of the love we should all have for God. This is the Supreme Law: *Listen O Israel, Yahweh our God is the one Yahweh. You shall love Yahweh your God with all your heart, with all your soul, and with all your strength. Let these words, I urge you today, be written on your heart* (Dt 6:4-9).

We Christians are united with Jesus as the branch is united to the vine. We are called to love not only our fellow Christians but all our non-Christian brothers and sisters as well. It is this spirit of love that pleases the Father. To live in this spirit is to be another Christ and to receive the Father's blessing.

In the New Testament we see that God favors Jesus and approves all that He teaches. For Christians, God's delight in Jesus is all that matters: *This is My Beloved Son, in Whom I take delight* (Mt 3:17). We accept the Old Testament as Jesus accepted it, and in the way He interpreted it. When we are troubled by passages in the Hebrew Bible which conflict with our Christian understanding today, we remember that Jesus, too, had problems with certain texts, and paid dearly for speaking out about them.

Holy Spirit, Soul of my soul, I adore You.
Guide me, strengthen me, console me.
Tell me what to do, give me Your orders, and
I promise to submit to whatever You desire of me,
And to accept everything You allow to happen to me.
Let me only know Your will.

(Cardinal Mercier)

(From M.E.C., no address)

God delights in me! Yes, it is amazing! And I've experienced this delight only recently, at age 58. Of course, I've known for a long time that God loves me and that His love is unconditional, that He loves me, "as I am," that in fact God is love. But knowing it, I mean intellectually, is light years away from real understanding, that is from realization.

I have nothing to tell you that I did that delighted God. It was simply a willingness for Him to come to my waiting, needful self. Maybe it was the very first time I was completely open to His coming. But He came and I knew He took delight in me. In His great mercy He allowed me to experience this joy (His joy) together with my own. I did nothing so there is no story to this; but anyway I am grateful. Pray for me that I may become more open, more ready, and that He may increase and I may decrease.

God's Love Is Personal

Because God's love for you is personal, He wants you to return His love in a personal way. Jesus said, *When you pray, do not imitate the hypocrites. They love to say their prayers . . . for people to see them. I tell you solemnly they have had their reward. When you pray, go to your private room and when you have shut the door, pray to your Father who is in that secret place. And your Father — who sees all that is done in secret — will reward you* (Mt 6:5-6).

Praying to the Father is a private matter. The Lord doesn't want us to make a show of it. Imagine a king talking to a subject who keeps turning around in the middle of every sentence to see who's observing the royal visit. The king would not be pleased.

The Lord's love is personal. When you address Him, then do it for His eyes only. When you go about doing good in the world, keep the same attitude in mind. He is very much aware of your noble intentions and desires. His affection for you is a given fact of life. Have no doubt about it. Your task is only to open yourself to Him. Playing to the crowd is insincere, immature, and disrespectful.

There are countless opportunities to be personal with the Lord. All it takes is a little imagination.

(From James R. Tallon, Howard Beach, NY)

Many, many years ago when I was young and the cares of the world weighed only lightly on my shoulders, I used to take extreme delight going Christmas shopping with my mother. One evening in particular stands out in my mind as though it happened yesterday.

Mom and I were in a store and she made a purchase. We left the store and had gone about a block or two when Mom stopped and exclaimed, "Oh dear, I don't have my package. I must have left it in the store." I told her to wait right there and I went back to find it. The package was nowhere around, so I purchased a duplicate, brought it to Mom and said, "Here it is. You left it on the counter." Down deep I had the feeling God must have chuckled because He knew it was not the same package.

Mom never said a word then, except for a grateful, "Thank you," but sometime after Christmas she said, "You bought another one, didn't you?" I pleaded innocent, but I knew God and Mom were pleased, and when I think of it, so was I. It is always a pleasure to delight God.

It doesn't matter if anyone else sees what you're about. What's important is that God sees it, and He smiles. You may not see His smile, but you can visualize it in your mind's eye.

St. John of the Cross asked one of his penitents, "Wherein does your prayer consist?" She replied, "In considering the beauty of God and in rejoicing that He has such beauty." St. John praised her for her answer. Was he being logical? After all, we know God is a pure Spirit and no one can look upon Him directly. And yet, we can certainly speak of His beauty. He is reflected in all that is beautiful, even the beauty of a human smile.

Last summer while vacationing in Combermere, Ontario,

Canada, I offered Mass for about 50 neighbors on the bank of the Madawaska River. A glorious July sunset lit up the sky, and children of all ages joined their parents and grandparents around an outdoor altar. Some of those attending were summer vacationers. The rest were native to the area.

One local family, the Mahons, accounted for nearly half of all those attending. After Mass, Tom Mahon, the 89-year-old, red-cheeked patriarch of the clan, sat next to me at the cookout. He was smiling broadly as he boasted of having 25 grandchildren and 22 great-grandchildren.

All through this happy conversation, one great-grandchild after another climbed up on his lap, only to scurry away a few seconds later. Tom just laughed and let each one come and go with a kiss or a pat on the head. He would probably be embarrassed to hear me say it, but for me, his smile was a perfect expression of God's radiant satisfaction with His children, *For the Lord takes delight in his people* (Ps 149:4).

If you think about it, the smile of God is more visible than you might think. We can see it reflected in the noble sentiments of our brothers and sisters everywhere. What's even more exciting, we can evoke it by loving one another. Being made in God's image, we not only belong to Him, we can reflect Him, we can think like Him, and we can love the way He loves: selflessly and unconditionally. In this intriguing relationship with God, we are able to offer ourselves to Him and become channels of His mercy. He can achieve His purpose through us. Nothing could be more personal.

When we make our self-offering in union with Christ, we are praying the prayer of the Church for the world. The Father insists that we do it for His eyes only. In His Sermon on the Mount, Jesus had much to say about how we should behave in God's sight: *When you fast,* he said, *do not put on a gloomy look as the hypocrites do. They put on long faces to let men know that*

they are fasting. I tell you solemnly, they have their reward. . . .
Rather, when you fast, put on festive clothing so that no one will
suspect you are hungry, except your Father who knows every
secret. And He will reward you (Mt 6:16-18). Jesus invites us to
be bright and cheerful, even in times of penance and mortifica-
tion. Why? Because He wants us to rejoice in all circumstances, even when we fast.

Fasting is a private matter. It's something that's between
the person fasting and Almighty God. Pope St. Leo the Great
commented on this passage: "What reward is Jesus referring to
when He says that those who put on long faces do it to be seen?
Isn't it human praise? Such a desire puts on a false mask of
respectability, for where there is no concern for conscience,
untruthful reputation gives pleasure. The result is that con-
cealed injustice enjoys a false reputation."

The Lord wants us to think first about how the Father will
see us, not how our neighbor will think of us. It delights the
Lord when we perform our hidden actions for Him alone. He
also likes it when we look directly into His eyes and ask Him
what He would like us to do for Him in the coming day.

I have spent most of my life trying to understand God. I
talk to Him. I talk about Him. And at times, I even dare to talk
for Him. All the while I am conscious of the fact that there is so
much about Him that I do not know. But Jesus gave us this
important piece of information: the Father does not want us to
play to the crowd. He wants us to do what we do, for His eyes
only. When we do, we begin to love God in a personal way —
not for what He can give us, but for Himself alone. This is the
highest   goal   of   asceticism.   And,   when   embraced
wholeheartedly, it awakens new joy in the soul. Cardinal
Suhard once wrote: "Joy is the infallible sign of the presence of
God." Joy is the natural condition of those who know that the
love of God enfolds them.

When we speak of God we are, of course, referring to the

Blessed Trinity. You and I have the privilege of sharing in the passionate love of God. This is a profound mystery, one well worth pondering.

On television, a detective mystery usually revolves around a case to be solved. In theology, a mystery is a sacred truth which will never be solved — or fully understood, for that matter. All we can do is benefit from what we know, and accept what we do not fully understand. The best that theologians can do is try to explain the facts that surround the mystery. This is another way of saying that they try to explain the unexplainable.

When we reach the limits of our understanding of any truth, most of us become a little frustrated, feeling as though we don't know anything at all. But we know a great deal. For instance, we know that God is One, and yet He is Three Divine Persons. We know the meaning of three and one, but together they seem to be incompatible in the same being. The notion of threeness and oneness only represent the facts that explain God's nature. They do not reveal His mystery to us.

While we have reams of theology books written about the mystery of God, hardly anything exists on the meaning of the word "mystery" itself. God's Being is veiled in mystery. And although the terms of the mystery, or the facts surrounding the doctrine, may be clear, the way they combine is not. Threeness and oneness do not compute.

Many theological controversies raged in the Church over the centuries, all attempting to clarify the teachings on Jesus. For instance, was He more man than God, or more God than man? Fortunately for us, the Church settled each controversy as it came along. In this case the formula to decide the controversy was this: Jesus Christ is true God and true man. There you have it. Or do you? What this teaching does is prevent us from exaggerating Christ's humanity to the point of minimizing His divinity, as the movie *Jesus Christ Superstar*

did, thus giving us a sentimental Jesus whose only real authority was in His own self-assurance. It keeps us, too, from
minimizing the role of human cooperation in the plan of redemption. Jesus was truly human.

The bishops of the world usually settle these debates at a
universal Church Council, and the theologians have to accept
the "Magisterium," the teaching authority of the pope united
with the bishops. Then the scholars discuss the implications of
the doctrine. For instance, if Jesus is true God, did He have a
superhuman mind? The answer is "No" because He was a true
human being. Needless to say, the importance of Mary's role in
cooperating in God's plan becomes evident.

Once the various debates on issues are settled in an
authoritative way, we have clarity about the terms of the
doctrine even though, fundamentally, the doctrine itself still
remains a mystery. It really doesn't matter if we do not fully
understand how Jesus could be both God and man. What
matters is that we know God became man. The Incarnation is
the central doctrine of our faith.

The Creator of the universe is not aloof. He loves us the
way a good and noble father loves his children, and more.
God's love is passionate. The Awesome One is also called the
Hound of Heaven.

Bringing this discussion down to earth, I'd like to share a
special letter with you. People understand God's fatherhood in
different ways. Here's one you may find interesting.

(From Victor Debono, Toronto, Canada)

*Ever since I was very young I always believed that God had
not only created the great minds, the persons who built the
beautiful cathedrals and discovered medical secrets which resulted in many miracles of healing, but that He also created*

*people like Charlie Chaplin, Lucille Ball and the like, because
he wanted us to laugh and be happy.*

*One day last summer I was sitting on my veranda when I
noticed two small boys, about three or four years old, trying
their utmost to ride a two-wheel bike. They pushed and pulled
each other, taking turns, to no avail as they always ended face
up with their rear to the ground. Finally one of them managed
to ride for a few feet. And with that they hugged, jumped and
clapped their hands for sheer joy. I laughed, too, and shared in
their happiness.*

*But the thought hit me: God Himself is probably laughing
and sharing His delight as I did in the two boys.*

I tend to agree with Victor. The Father enjoys what He
loves. We delight Him at times, even without realizing it.

Jesus asked us to have a childlike faith. We should never
allow ourselves to become skeptics or cynics. Those who put
their trust in the teachings of Jesus are the beneficiaries of this
marvelous knowledge we call the good news of the Gospel: God
is Unchanging Love. He pursues those whom He loves, and He
wants them to respond to His love with childlike confidence.

(From R.B., no address)

*It has always been fairly easy for me to help people without
feeling it was extra special. Then a neighbor had a fall which
resulted in a serious arm injury. When the cast was removed she
needed a good deal of therapy. She asked me to take her to each
session and wait for her, then drive her home. Since she wasn't
my favorite person and I wasn't anxious to do it, I told Jesus that
this would be His Christmas gift from me.*

*Therapy sessions mounted up and a strange thing hap-
pened. She was nicer than I anticipated and we had many fine*

hours together. However, after numerous weeks, Christmas was drawing near and I had not done my chores for my large family. I told God I was happy to give Him this gift, but now I was concerned about my own duties. Within the hour the phone rang. My neighbor said she thought she would try to manage to drive herself. Jesus was telling me He was pleased with my gift and it was sufficient.

It takes a childlike faith to imagine Jesus interacting with you when you offer your gifts to Him. All of this may sound like nonsense to skeptics, but those with faith know better.

Scientists, by and large, are among the most entrenched skeptics on earth when it comes to supernatural mysteries. They shouldn't be because they deal with mystery all the time, exploring the unknown, peeling away more and more layers of human ignorance with each new discovery. Yet they never solve the central mystery: How did the universe get here in the first place, and what is our role in it?

I have been exchanging letters for a few years with a well-known astronomer who will not admit that the universe must have a prime mover, a first cause. He simply says, "Why do we need a cause?" Scientists know that every effect has a cause. They work on experiments all the time looking for the explanation behind certain phenomena. And yet, when we apply the same principle to the cosmos, postulating that there must be a Supreme Intelligence behind created intelligence, many of them repeat the same dreary refrain, "Why do we have to have a cause? The Big Bang theory is sufficient enough to explain where we came from."

I'm afraid that's not good enough. What caused the Big Bang? That is the mystery science has not solved, and probably never will. Every school child knows that something doesn't come from nothing. Why, then, is it difficult for some adults to accept the idea of a Supreme Intelligence behind the created universe? And — going one step further — why would anyone question the idea that an intelligent being has personality?

Nothing emanates from God's life that is not personal. In this context the words of Jesus, challenging us to believe in Him, have a special force: *Unless you become as a little child, you cannot enter the Kingdom of heaven* (Lk 18:17).

When it comes to God's life, we do well to accept the things we do know, and work with them. Even though we are at different levels in our capacity to understand God, each one of us has enough information right now to become God's personal lover, and to rejoice in that love.

You are God's bliss. Claim His love, and you will begin to experience it.

Heavenly Father, teach me to live for your eyes only.
Help me to appreciate the mystery of Your loving presence,
And give me the grace to love You with my whole heart
and mind and soul. Amen.

(From Christiana Sokolski, Welland, Ontario)

God, my Father, has given me the greatest, most complete joy that no person could give me. His love and gifts are everywhere. I know in my heart and soul that He has been with me all the 38 years of my life, and even before I was born. He was with me through my abusive childhood, my sinful youth and my marriage to an alcoholic husband as I was trying to raise two small children to love God, their own father and all people.

God, in the Holy Trinity, was there to show me that hope is everyone's salvation, that there is great joy in the face of great sadness. Our Father always has an answer for every problem. I know because I trust God, love Him and have prayed to Him along with many others.

My family is reconciled, my husband has found sobriety through A.A. and my children are the greatest gift God has given me besides His Son and the Holy Spirit.

There are many lessons to be learned in suffering. Forgiveness is one of the greatest gifts one human being can give to another, and it truly delights our Father in heaven. Thank you for allowing me to write.

CHAPTER THREE

God's Love Is Real Love

In His final discourse, Jesus explained His purpose on earth: to give glory to the Father, and to give eternal life to those the Father entrusted to Him: *Father, the hour has come: glorify Your Son, so that Your Son may glorify You; and through the power over all mankind that You have given Him, let Him give eternal life to all those You have entrusted to Him. Eternal life is this: to know You, the only true God, and Jesus Christ whom You have sent. Father, I have given You glory on earth by finishing the work You have given Me to do* (Jn 17:1-4).

God's love always seeks the good of the person loved, and He rejoices in that good. The love of God is an unselfish love. He does not seek our love for His own advantage. Christ's sacrificial death taught us that God willingly surrenders self-interest to help us. He is always there for us, working little miracles to help us cope.

His love is universal. It extends even to the wicked. Jesus forgave those who persecuted Him. He urged us to do the same. *Love your enemies* (Mt 5:44). Even if we are not able to love our enemies, at least we can try. No one is outside of God's embrace.

God's love is efficacious. That means it produces good fruit. It is not merely passive, like the benevolence of some remote king. God takes the initiative in drawing us to Himself: *He sent His only begotten Son* (Jn 3:16).

God gives each of us a mission. If we perform it well, our life will glorify the Father. At the Christophers we always stress the fact that each one of us has a job to do in this world that no one else can do. Each of us has a particular cross fitted to our back that no one else can carry.

In Chapter 17 of St. John's Gospel, Jesus explains that His whole ministry was to communicate the Father's name (v. 6) and to teach us that eternal life is found in knowing the Father and experiencing Him in faith (v. 8). Jesus explains why He went all over preaching the Good News: *I have told them many things while I was with them so that they would be filled with My joy* (v. 13).

Then the Lord prayed that His followers *may be made perfectly one, as You Father are in Me, and I in You . . . I pray that they may be one in Us that the world might believe that You sent Me . . . and that You loved them as You loved Me* (vv. 21, 23).

He assures us that the holiness of His followers will manifest itself in the way they show love for one another. This love will be a reflection of the Father's love in them: *This is My command: love one another as I have loved you* (Jn 15:12).

The following excerpt is from the writings of Mechtild of Magdeburg (c. 1210-1285). From her early childhood she received the most extraordinary mystical graces. In 1230 she joined a religious community called the Beguines and remained there for 40 years. Her extraordinary vocation eventually aroused jealousy and she was forced to withdraw from Magdeburg to a convent in Helfta. Her mystical experiences are recorded in her book, *The Flowering Light of the Godhead*, which takes the form of a dialogue between herself and Christ.

Soul

Ah dearest Love, for how long
Have you lain in wait for me?
What, O what can I do?
I am hunted, captured, bound,
Wounded so terribly
That never can I be healed.
Cunning blows have you dealt,
Shall I ever recover from you?

Love (Jesus Christ)

I hunted you for my pleasure,
I caught you for my desire,
I bound you for my joy,
Your wounds have made us one,
My cunning blows made me yours.
I drove Almighty God
From heaven and it was I
Who took His human life
And gave Him back again
With honor to His Father —
How could you hope, poor one,
To save yourself from me?

Here we see something of Mechtild's understanding of happiness: to be devoured by her mystical spouse. This passage tells us that we are not only God's delight, we are the object of His desire.

What follows is a true story told by a missionary priest just back from Africa after five years abroad.

I had studied long and hard to learn the language of the native people. It took me more than three years to become comfortable in normal, everyday conversation. One day after

*preaching at Mass on Sunday, one of the men came up to me
and said, "Father, you are good to come this long distance to
teach us about God, but you seem to have a different idea about
Him than we have. You seem to search for God with a telescope.
It is as though you see your prey at a distance, but never get close
enough to capture Him. We think of God differently. For us, it is
more like the tiger hunting for food. Once he charges and leaps
on his prey, the chase is over. Only, for us, the tiger is God. We
are the prey. God has already landed and claimed us."*

The missionary began to see things differently after that
conversation. He remembered the poem, "The Hound of
Heaven," by Francis Thompson (1859-1907), which expres-
ses the same powerful insight: God is the hunter and we are the
hunted.

Catherine de Vinck in her poem, "In the Naked Place,
The Eagle Feeds," compares God to a bird of prey:

> *Where language ends*
> > *words die of thirst*
> > *in huge savannahs of loneliness.*
> *The hands of the clock wither*
> > *time stops*
> *when we reach that outer point*
> > *beyond the knowledge of leaf and rock.*
> *We say nothing:*
> > *who could understand?*
>
> *Without questions, without answers*
> > *naked to the bones*
> *what is there to explain?*
> > *Maybe the voice of rain*
> > *the small palpitation of crickets*
> > *or the mute sound of stones*
> > *could speak about what is happening.*
> *Nowhere to hide, no safe-conduct*

no passport to a country of meadows and roses.
The land is dense, opaque, flat
with neither ridge nor hollow.

From infinite heights, the eagle falls
falls upon its prey; we are grasped
torn apart, consumed:
at last our heart opens
gives forth its blood.

God's love is awesome and we are the object of His desire. He is an all-consuming Fire and in Him we return to dust, only to rise again from our ashes like the Phoenix.

In the Eucharist, we consume God under the appearances of bread and wine in a union of love. However, we often forget that God wants to devour us as well. This is the language of poets. The "devouring" refers more to the passion of lovers than the feast of kings. The passion of lovers is a mutual pleasure, freely bestowed from one to another. God does not take anyone's freedom away. He waits until we are hungry for Him.

God has often been misunderstood. In Medieval spiritual literature there was a strong emphasis put on suffering. It was as though the minute you give yourself to God, He puts you on the rack. That is a totally false understanding of love. Love is only interested in the good of the beloved. Love is patient, kind and humble. The Lord came on earth not to crucify us but to bring us joy. The cross is a real part of our faith. But we see it as a blessing in disguise. Christ's suffering was not only the sign of His surrender to the Father's will; it was also the coin used to purchase our redemption.

The ultimate meaning of revelation, therefore, is not suffering but joy. Jesus died that we might live. He allowed Himself to be devoured by the Living God so that the whole human race would be freed to receive His eternal glory.

The notion of sacrificial love is more manageable when we reduce it to life-size proportions. For instance, a mother who gives up her sleep to care for a sick child is rewarded when the child gets well, even if the child forgets to say, "Thank you." Her joy is in the loving. She doesn't count the loss of sleep as a sacrifice. She sees it as her natural duty — in fact, as a privilege.

God's love is like that. He doesn't count the cost, nor does He ask for your permission to care for you. He simply loves because He is love. The saints had a deep understanding of this wonderful truth.

St. Francis of Assisi was born in Italy in 1182 and, after a carefree youth, he renounced his inheritance and surrendered to the call of God by devoting himself to a life of poverty. He attracted many followers, and today several religious communities, consisting of thousands of priests, religious and lay people have adopted his rule and his spirit.

Francis did not record his most intimate experiences with the Lord as many mystics have done. But he wrote the following piece at the turn of the twelfth century: *The Father willed that His blessed and glorious Son, whom He gave to us and who was born for us, should through His own blood, offer Himself as a sacrificial victim on the altar of the cross. This was done not for Himself, through whom all things were made, but for us and our sins. And He desires all of us to be saved through Him and to receive Him with pure heart and chaste body.*

St. Francis was blessed with abundant graces in his lifetime. He had a pure heart, and after his death in 1226 he was rewarded with a spiritual legacy extending far beyond his wildest dreams.

One of the many admirers of St. Francis was born centuries later. Juan de Yepes y Alvarez first saw the light of day at Fontiveros, Spain in 1542. He is now known to us as St. John of the Cross. Juan was a contemplative, a theologian and a poet. At the age of 21 he joined the Carmelite Order and was ordained a priest in 1567.

Though he was only five feet tall, St. Teresa of Avila saw him as a spiritual giant. She once wrote another Prioress about him, "You have a great treasure in that holy man . . . Our Lord has given him a special grace . . . He is very spiritual and of great experience and learning." Teresa was 51 and Juan was 25 when they met. He soon became her confessor. She called him "Little Seneca" because of his short stature and great wisdom.

When St. Teresa began the reform of her religious community of women, she enlisted Fray Juan's aid, asking him to work for the reform of the Carmelite Order of men. He accepted the challenge and gathered a reform-minded group around him, urging a return to the strict rule. John of the Cross founded the Discalced Carmelites. "Discalced" means "without shoes."

Naturally there was resistance to his efforts and he soon suffered the rejection and humiliation that nearly every reformer and founder of a religious community experiences. Juan was actually imprisoned within his own monastery walls by members of his community. He died neglected and scorned in Pignuel, Spain, in 1591. It wasn't until 1726 that he was canonized a saint, and in 1926 Pope Pius XI declared him a doctor of the Church.

Much of St. John's mystical poetry was written during his imprisonment. Here is an example:

> *O flame of living love.*
> *That dost eternally*
> *Pierce through my soul with so consuming heat.*
> *Since there's no help above,*
> *Make thou an end of me,*
> *And break the bond of this encounter sweet.*

> *O burn that burns to heal!*
> *O more than pleasant wound!*
> *And O soft hand, O touch most delicate,*
> *That does new life reveal.*
> *That dost in grace abound,*
> *And, slaying, dost from death to life translate.*

St. John loved God passionately. In citing him, however, I do not want to give the impression that only the most extraordinary souls are blessed by God with mystical graces, or that they alone are asked to carry heavy crosses. It often happens that ordinary people carry extraordinary crosses with great courage and nobility.

(From Terry Ann Modica, Jackson, NJ)

I am aware of God's delight in me, and the best way to stay in touch with His good feelings toward me is to take time every day to communicate with Him. I pray to align myself with Him and I read the Bible to be reminded of how much He loves me.

I went through a period, however, of thinking God was angry with me and not pleased at all with me. A friend had pointed out a flaw in my personality, and she said God wanted her to tell me about it. I began to see myself as unworthy of God's delight. He was a scolding Daddy and it was impossible to please Him because I could not be perfect.

After a few days of crying and self-belittlement, it finally dawned on me that I should ask God to help me sort through what my friend had said. It was difficult to ask because I feared He might berate me for my imperfections. But I decided to trust His Parenthood. The moment I asked for His help, my thinking began to change.

God took special delight in me then because I wanted to

trust Him in spite of my feelings. Turning to Him allowed me to draw near to Him. He wrapped me in His loving arms and gently stroked my mind. It was then that I realized God does not point out my flaws to other people and instruct them to inform me of them. When He corrects, it is through inner conviction. It does not result in confusion and self-belittlement and wrong perceptions about God. His corrections result in a sense of inner peace. His is a small, still voice inside my heart, not the voice of a friend who has a problem with my personality.

I like Terry's opening line: ". . . the best way to stay in touch with His good feelings toward me is to take time every day to communicate with Him." We need prayer to keep the right spirit alive.

There are many saints and mystics who can explain God's love far better than I. May I introduce you to St. Bonaventure, the Prince of Mystics.

St. Bonaventure was born about 1218. He studied philosophy and theology in Paris and, as a follower of St. Francis of Assisi, became the Minister General of the Franciscan Order. He was elevated to the rank of Cardinal-Bishop of Albano, and he died at the Council of Lyons in 1274.

In his work, *The Journey of the Mind to God,* he gives us this insight: "Christ is both the way and the door. Christ is the staircase and the vehicle, like the throne of mercy . . . the mystery hidden from all ages."

In his work, *Mystical Opuscula,* which was translated by José de Vinck, St. Bonaventure writes about the seven steps by which the sweetness of God's love is attained: watchfulness, comforting trust, inflaming desire, uplifting rapture, joyful peace, transporting happiness, and perfect intimacy. He says you must proceed with each step in the order he has outlined if you wish to attain perfect charity.

Here is his advice on carrying out your desire to love God:

One, since the Spouse is at hand, watchfulness must keep you alert so you might exclaim: O God my God, for Thee do I watch at break of day . . . my soul has desired Thee in the night.

Two, since the Spouse is faithful, trust must be your comfort, so that you may exclaim: In Thee, O Lord, have I hoped, let me never be confounded, and with Job: Slay me though He might, I will wait for Him.

Three, since the Spouse is sweet, desire must inflame you, so that you may exclaim: As the deer longs for the running waters, so my soul longs for you, O God.

Four, since the Spouse is lofty, rapture must uplift you, so that you may exclaim: How lovely is Your dwelling place, O Lord of hosts!

Five, since the Spouse is beautiful, delight in Him must bring you peace, so that you may exclaim with the bride: My lover belongs to me, and I to Him.

Six, since the Spouse is rich, you must be filled with happiness, so that you may exclaim: When cares abound within me, Your comfort gladdens my soul.

Seven, since the love of the Spouse is strong, close intimacy must weld you to Him, so that you may exclaim: For me, to be near God is my good, and also who shall separate us from the love of Christ? (Op. cit., "The Triple Way, Or Love Enkindled," Chapter Three, Subsection C).

Of all the words St. Bonaventure has written the ones that touch me deepest are these: *No matter how well we plan our spiritual progress, nothing comes of it unless divine assistance intervenes. And divine assistance is there for those who seek it, humbly and overtly, who sigh for it in this vale of tears by fervent prayer. Prayer, then, is the mother and the beginning of the ascent to the Trinity.*

Reading St. Bonaventure is worth the effort. Irenaeus, an early Church Father, once said, *God's greatest glory is man fully alive.* St. Bonaventure was certainly fully alive.

God our Father wants us to be happy with Him for all eternity, beginning now. Therefore, trust your imagination. Visualize the whole range of gifts God has waiting for you, surprises planned for you from all eternity: the healing of broken relationships; a brand new, healthy body; peace of soul; and a rich enjoyment of God Himself. He will bring you the fullness of life because He loves you and He wants your happiness.

God is a passionate lover.

> O gentle Father,
> Help me to believe in your love,
> in good times and bad.
> Teach me to seek and find you,
> that I may love you,
> not for what you can do for me,
> but for Yourself alone.

(From Ed Neumann, Brooksville, FL)

As one of those people with "messy lives," I decided to do something about it. After 46 years of making a mess, and 30 years without going to church, I ended up broke and alone — or so it seemed — until a Catholic friend in Ohio told me I needed to pray. I wasn't too receptive. After all, I was raised a Protestant. What would a Catholic know?

Some disappointing times with "my" Church in earlier years prevented me from wanting to go back. However, a few nights later things got real bad. I knew I needed help, fast! I, who denied the Church for so long was in trouble. Guilt, anger, loneliness, fear, self-pity, hatred, confusion and despair were all out of control. I took my friend's advice and walked into St. Anthony's church in Brooksville. I waited to see if a priest might walk by, but they were busy. Twice I turned to leave. The second time I passed a small statue of the Holy Mother. I paused, and I felt she welcomed me. I lit a candle, fell to my knees and for the first time in my life, really prayed.

I'm in the process of change, growing in faith and hope. I know I have been forgiven — forgiving myself was the hardest part. I am taking instructions at St. Anthony's now; gosh, when you feel this good, why change? Just go for more! Oh, yes. My Catholic "friend" in Ohio is my ex-wife. We found we are still in love with each other. With the grace of God we will be able to make that love grow, and maybe . . . well, I know prayer works!

CHAPTER FOUR

God Loves The Sinner

If a man has a hundred sheep, and one wanders away and is lost, what will he do? Won't he leave the ninety-nine others and go out into the hills to search for the lost one? And if he finds it, he will rejoice over it more than over the ninety-nine others safe at home! Just so, it is not my Father's will that even one of these little ones should perish (Mt 18:13).

God loves the sinner. And who among us is not a sinner? We are all prone to human weakness. But what a wonderful discovery it is to realize that God pursues those who are most in need of His mercy.

The seven deadly sins are all different forms of the one sin of selfishness. *Pride*: I want to outrank you and surpass you in every way. *Greed*: I want more possessions, and don't try to stop me. *Envy*: I want what you have. *Lust*: I want more sex. *Anger*: I want my own way. *Gluttony*: I want more to eat, more to drink, more to shoot up. *Sloth*: I want to be left alone; don't bother me.

Each one of these vices can become a tenacious enemy of the soul, but with God's grace they can all be conquered. If any one of them is allowed to grow out of control, mortal injury to the soul will result. All of the deadly sins lead to interpersonal difficulties. When left uncorrected, these in turn cause broken relationships, resentment and even hatred.

(From Ohio)

My life became a nightmare. From the time I was twelve or thirteen I collected pornography and gradually became more involved with my own lust. As an adult, I spent thousands of dollars every year on prostitutes and could only be described as a sexual addict. With the help of a priest, I found my way back to God and discovered Sexaholics Anonymous. They are similar to Alcoholics Anonymous — in fact they use the same Twelve-Step Program. It made all the difference. With the help of God, I've been chaste for the last five years.

I petition the Lord each night, as my final prayer before going to bed, to grant me a safe and peaceful rest of mind and body and soul, free from all sin and temptation and anxiety as I wait in joyful hope for the coming of my Savior, Jesus Christ. And when I rise in the morning, I ask God to give me a more fervent desire to know, love and serve Him with my whole mind, body and heart, and to love my neighbor as I love myself and as Jesus loves me. These prayers were inspired out of my own great need for His protection all through the day and night.

I have never faltered as long as I have said my prayers. I give Jesus the credit, for He is the source of my strength. Even so, I can't help feeling that He is pleased with my progress so far. Please pray for me.

Progress begins when you decide to turn to God. In the case of lust, it also helps to realize you can't put out a fire with dry wood. Certain steps must be taken to avoid temptation. In that context, if you see God as a friend who will come through for you, and if you think of yourself as a saint-in-the-making, you'll spare yourself a lot of unnecessary guilt. A positive frame of mind is important if you are going to carry through with your good intentions. Changes will begin to take place in ways you never thought possible.

Sexuality is such a basic part of human life that it deserves special mention. It is a gift, not a curse. Like fire, it must be used with great care because it can burn you and others. The awesome power of sexuality is given for the noble purpose of bringing children into the world. Sexuality also fosters the love between spouses which is needed to help them to stay together. In raising the children God sends them, they need to become less selfish and more selfless, putting their children before themselves. The goal is to create in the home an atmosphere of emotional comfort for one and all.

A healthy sexuality enables us to see the beauty of the opposite sex, and to enjoy the glow of that beauty. At the same time we need to pray for the grace of chastity. Chastity is the virtue that regulates the expression of human love.

The human body is the masterpiece of God's material universe. Apart from its physical beauty, it dazzles the imagination with its interdependent systems, harmoniously organized into one perfect whole.

The circulatory system, the respiratory system, the digestive system, the reproductive system, are all wonderfully designed to achieve their own purposes within a balanced unity.

Reproduction touches on the nervous system. Males and females, normally rational and reserved are drawn to intimacy and passion by the force of their own nature. Beginning with the power of attraction, culminating in a surrender of love, followed by conception and the birth of a child, the human body astounds us with its mysterious powers.

He made man to His own image . . . male and female He made them . . . and He blessed them saying "increase and multiply."

God knew what He was doing when He made the reproductive system. He looked upon all that He had made and *He saw that it was good.* God gave human beings the freedom to use or abuse these powers. He asked them to order their lives, their loves, and their daily activity so that everything would be done according to His design. This takes into account certain rules: rules of God, rules of society, and rules of conscience.

Even though some people in today's world may dispute the rules, they cannot escape the fact that God wants them to live in the light, honorably and responsibly. The essential purpose of the reproductive system is the reproduction of human life. The abuse of this faculty often results in misery, chaos, and even murder.

One does not have to be religious to see the wisdom of avoiding the path that leads to abortion, or AIDS, or ruined reputation. One ought to strive for chastity to regulate human love. More is at stake than earthly happiness.

One day we will all stand before God in self-knowledge, and in the full realization of what our Redeemer did to save us. Hopefully, we will be able to stand there with great pride, knowing that we tried to use the gift of procreation well; that even despite occasional failures, we were mindful of our obligation: to cherish the gift; to cherish ourselves; and to cherish the other person to whom we were attracted.

There's a great quote in Dostoyevsky's *The Brothers Karamazov* which can be helpful to those discouraged about their weakness. Wise and gentle Father Zossima speaks these priestly words: *Do not despair. It's enough that you are distressed . . . I believe you are sincere and good . . . Above all, avoid falseness of every kind, especially falseness to yourself. Watch over your deceitfulness . . . what seems to be bad within you will grow purer from the very fact of your observing it in yourself. Avoid fear. Never be frightened of your own faint-heartedness in attaining love. Don't be frightened, even of your own evil actions.*

These words give us a glimpse of the kind-heartedness of God. Holiness is possible because God's love is unfailing. He is at work all the time, molding and shaping us into a new creation. He is the master artist; we are the clay in His hands. There are times in the process when the clay is a mess. Don't judge the potter too quickly.

The prophet Jeremiah once reported what the Lord said to him: *"Get up and make your way down to the potter's house. There I shall let you hear what I have to say." So Jeremiah went to observe the potter at work. Whenever anything went wrong, the potter would start afresh to work the clay into the shape he wanted, as potters do. As the prophet was watching, this word was spoken to him by the Lord: "House of Israel, cannot I do to you what this potter does? — it is the Lord who speaks. Yes, clay is in the potter's hand, so you are in mine"* (18:16).

God asks that we be pliable and open to His inspiration, open to His love. He is molding us for a destiny of eternal happiness. By our union with Christ and our cooperation in His plan, we will gradually take shape into something much more beautiful than we could have imagined. We have the power to please and delight God by allowing Him to mold us. Let us never be discouraged if we're not yet where we want to be. The saints had problems too. *I am most happy to boast about my weakness*, St. Paul wrote, *and I'm glad to be a living demonstration of Christ's power over me. I am content with weakness, insults, hardships, persecutions and difficulties for Christ's sake. For when I am weak, then I am strong* (2 Cor 12:9).

God must love the sinner, He made so many of us!

Weakness comes in a variety of forms. Each of us has a different problem to contend with. Some have a combination of weaknesses. Far from judging us, Jesus wanted so much to help us. After His resurrection, He said to Peter, *Feed my lambs, feed my lambs, feed my little sheep.* Imagine yourself as one of His sheep. In spite of your frailty, and perhaps because of it, you are precious to the Lord. He doesn't want to lose you. He wants you fed and cared for. He offers you the Bread of Life, His own Body and Blood.

Peter understood that Jesus asked for a lifetime commitment. And, however faltering his steps, he gladly accepted
the challenge. He went to Rome — probably against the
advice of his family — and preached Christ crucified, incurring the wrath of those in power. He was arrested and condemned to die on the cross. Feeling unworthy to be crucified
as Jesus was, Peter asked to be hung upside down. Remember his words to Jesus: *Depart from me, Lord, for I am a
sinful man* (Lk 5:8).

The epistles of Peter are among the most exquisite in the
Bible. They are simple, direct and full of wisdom. We read
from his First Letter: *Each of you has received a special grace.
So, like good stewards responsible for all these different graces
of God, put yourselves at the service of others. If you are a
speaker, speak in words which seem to come from God; if you are
a helper, help as though every action was done at God's orders,
so that in everything God may receive the glory through Jesus
Christ* (4:10-11).

God asks us to help others through love and forgiveness.
Peter put it this way, *Charity overcomes a multitude of sins* (1 P
4:8). Since charity begins at home, it is so important to forgive
oneself. Real forgiveness is rooted in self-acceptance. Only
when we accept ourselves, can we rise to accept the human-
ness of others.

St. Therese of Lisieux once wrote that if it weren't for
God's grace she would have been the greatest sinner in the
world. I wonder what dark thoughts prompted her to make such
a statement? No doubt she realized that if she didn't control her
thoughts she would be in deep trouble.

A kind of cabin fever builds up in a contemplative
monastery. Therese was living in a building with no central
heating; the sisters never had a day off; there was never a sound
of laughter from children playing. The monotony of the solemn
silence must have been deafening. Learning to control her

thoughts in such an environment was essential to her mental health.

What she did was quite simple. She performed the duties of her state in life as faithfully and lovingly as she could, and turned everything else over to Jesus, trusting that He would make up for her shortcomings. She made charity her goal in life, offering acts of love as little flowers — one of the reasons she is often referred to as "The Little Flower" — to be placed at the feet of the Lord. Her autobiography reveals her simplicity, but we seldom advert to the price she paid to overcome her weaknesses.

My point is this: If someone as innocent as St. Therese could fear her own sinfulness, and if St. Peter considered himself an unworthy sinner, it's no wonder the rest of us get upset about our human condition. We are not so different from the saints after all. Like us, they were far from perfect, and they'd be the first to admit it. Biographers do us a disservice when they present the saints as icons instead of struggling human beings.

Let's be straightforward. We are human and we know it. But we also know that with God's grace, all things are possible. His grace converts us into saints-in-training. Sometimes the ones who look most like saints are really the villains. And often some pretty seedy looking individuals turn out to be saints.

The apostles couldn't always tell either. St. John once said to Jesus, *Master, we saw a man who is not one of us casting out devils in your name; and, because he is not one of us, we tried to stop him.* Jesus replied, *You must not stop him! No one who works miracles in my name is likely to speak evil of me. Anyone who is not against us is for us* (Mk 9:38-40).

There is a sense of urgency in Christ's words: *You must not stop him!* It's as though he were saying, "We need everyone we can get!" His tone reminds us that Jesus was human. He had needs. He needed the apostles to be loyal to Him. He

needed them to help Him to build up the Kingdom. He asked
them to stop being petty, reminding them to be respectful of the
workings of the Holy Spirit. Wherever and whenever the Spirit
is active, there the Church is being built up into a new and
glorious Kingdom.

There are two kinds of charismatic gifts in the Church: the
objective charisms of office, represented by the popes and
bishops (this is the authority structure of the Church), and the
personal, *subjective charisms* of individuals who, by their
prayers and good works, build up the Church. Jesus needs
both, and He tells us so. Jesus needs sinners, because there is
no one out there who is not a sinner. And if He doesn't have us,
whom does He have?

When I use the word "needy" in relation to Jesus, I do so
intentionally. It is difficult for many Christians to imagine Him
being in need. And yet, wasn't He afraid in the Garden of
Olives on the night He was arrested? We are conditioned to
think of Him as being above vulnerability and fear. But He was
human. He was sorely tempted to hate His enemies, but He
never did. Even though He is a Divine Person, He is also a
fully human one. He suffered the bitter humiliation of being
rejected by the very people He tried to help.

It is through His agony in the garden that we come to know
Him best. He was lonely and fearful the night they came to
arrest Him. Jesus needed human support then. And He still
needs His followers today to cooperate with Him in the plan of
redemption. We are all part of the overall solution, even
though we still have problems of our own.

How does one rise to the challenge of coming to His aid?

Certainly, one way is by not putting yourself down. If God
is for you, who can be against you? Never think of yourself as a
victim, or a poor helpless creature. There is always grace.
Jesus wants you to be a healer. You are another Christ, a
servant of the Father.

When Philip asked Jesus to show him the Father, Jesus answered with a tinge of disappointment in His voice: *Have I been with you all this time, Philip, and still you do not know Me? To have seen Me is to have seen the Father* (Jn 14:9).

Jesus' spirit of forgiveness is an expression of the Father's mercy. Love endures all things, and forgives all things. Jesus longed for His followers to put their faith in Him. Those who returned His love with a living faith, like Peter, were rewarded. The fact that Peter was a struggling sinner, who was capable of denying Him in a moment of weakness, did not concern Him. The important thing was Peter's willingness to go forth and preach the Good News.

Go and learn what this means: "I desire mercy, and not sacrifice." I have come to call sinners and not the just (Mt 9:13). We are like St. Peter. We're not much without God's grace. But with it, we can overcome the world.

> Father, thank you for your love.
> Thank you for seeing the good in me
> before I see it in myself.
> Help me to believe more deeply
> in Your unfailing mercy, and
> teach me to be an instrument
> of your love and peace.

(From Rose Krzyston, Cocoa, FL)

I am delighted to share with you the joy of God's love that I received the day I asked a friend to forgive me.

Prior to this event, I was getting continual nudges within me to forgive my long lost friend. After struggling with this, I decided just to go to her and ask her to forgive me. It was a beautiful reunion and that day changed my life. My new found friend helped me to discover another lost friend, the Third Person of the Blessed Trinity, the Holy Spirit. She had been praying to the Holy Spirit for our friendship to be restored.

Learning to forgive not only opens the door to let in God's love, but it also sets a prisoner free. And that prisoner was me.

Forgiveness is God's free gift to us. Ask for it.

CHAPTER FIVE

God Delights In Loving You

Each of the saints in heaven had a different approach to God. St. Francis of Assisi had a special fondness for seeing Him in nature, in the sun, the moon, the birds and the flowers. He called all living things his brothers and sisters. St. John of the Cross composed love poems to Almighty God. St. Therese, the Little Flower, often thought of herself as a baby in the arms of her Divine Father. There are countless saints who were given special insights into God's personality.

One of my favorites is a woman who lived at the turn of the 15th century, Blessed Julian of Norwich. She is known today only through her book, *Revelations of Divine Love*. Julian had a gift for understanding God's inner life of love. *We are His bliss*, she said, *He endlessly delights in us.*

She lived as a hermit in a cell attached to the church of St. Julian (hence her name) in the city of Norwich, England. Her reputation for holiness spread abroad. At about the age of thirty, she became deathly sick. In her delirium, she clung to the crucifix. Suddenly she was completely healed. Her pain vanished, and from that day on she began having mystical experiences: *I saw that God's love was behind everything He has done or will do; thus I learned that love was Our Lord's meaning.*

Her writings intrigued me! One of Julian's statements that caught my attention was her famous line: *The greatest honor we can give to Almighty God is to live gladly because of the knowledge of His love.* I wrote a book entitled *Enjoy the Lord* (NY: Alba House, 1988) to expand on that simple idea. Julian believed that the Gospel calls us to joy, not as an ideal but as a Christian duty. I found this idea captivating.

I had been raised in the thirties and forties when the gloom and doom school of spirituality was uncontested. I remember feeling trapped in a dark complex of ideas which made religion an awesome burden. Though I was never a scrupulous person, I must admit I was more afraid of God than in love with Him.

My struggle to attract His love was made even more difficult by my secret fear that He was not easy to please. In time I began to grow weary of religion. I thought God was testing me all the time. The harder I tried, the less satisfied I became with myself.

After awhile I had sense enough to realize I was on the wrong track. I prayed and gradually worked my way into a more trusting frame of mind. However, it wasn't until I discovered the writings of Julian of Norwich that I was able to articulate my own developing intuition that God wanted me to be happy. I realized that all the do's and don'ts of moral theology are there to guide me to happiness.

Julian's writings sparked my imagination with fresh hope, opening new insights: *It is God's will that we have true delight with Him in our salvation. And in it He wants us to be greatly comforted and strengthened. So, joyfully, He wishes our souls to be occupied by His grace. We are His bliss, because He endlessly delights in us; and so with His grace shall we delight in Him* (NY: Paulist Press, *The Classics of Western Spirituality*, "Showings," pp. 218-219).

In another section she writes about the art of giving:

. . . always the cheerful giver pays only little attention to the thing which he is giving, but all his desire . . . is to please and comfort the one to whom he is giving it. She then refers to the fact that Jesus gave His life as a ransom for the sins of the world. He wanted each one of us to come to a knowledge of the truth and be saved. Salvation, therefore, is a gift that one has the power to accept or reject. She continues, *And if the receiver accepts the gift gladly and gratefully, then the courteous giver counts as nothing all his expense and his labor, because . . . he has pleased and delighted the one whom he loves* (Op. cit., pp. 219-220).

"All the expense and labor," indeed! The passion and death of Christ are very much a part of Julian's thinking. Love and the cross are always connected in her writings: *I saw three longings in God,* she writes. *The first is that He longs to teach us to know Him, and to love Him always more and more, as is suitable and profitable to us. The second is that He longs to bring us up into His bliss, as souls are when taken out of pain into heaven. The third is to fill us with bliss . . . to last forever* (Ibid. p. 326).

Julian taught me what it means to believe in God's love with an unwavering faith. She made it all so real. I had always been aware that God is love, but somehow I didn't grasp the full significance of it. I'm sure I still don't, but I now appreciate the wonder of it more than I ever have in my entire life.

St. Cyril of Alexandria was asked to explain the way the Holy Spirit acts in our lives. He said the Holy Spirit is like the rain falling everywhere the same, and giving nourishment to everything it touches. As each plant receives the rain, it grows according to its own nature, producing its own particular fruit. We are like the plants and trees. As God showers His blessings upon each one of us, He nourishes us, and we mature in holiness according to our own specific nature and vocation. We are all given the same opportunity to flourish in His love.

(From Washington, DC)

This is such a little thing I've hesitated to write about it. But since the thought will not leave me, I've decided to do so.

Some years ago, I had a very unfriendly neighbor with a most unattractive personality. In her final illness, I went to see her in the hospital. She had lived alone, never married, and had no friends. In this first visit she looked so frightened and alone that my heart went out to her. It seemed to me this was a woman who had never been loved. I did everything I could think of to convince her that I cared for her. It wasn't much, but I held her hand, smoothed her forehead and spoke to her in a loving tone of voice. I really did care.

During that time I could sense her responding with love and almost joy. She only lasted about two weeks.

My hope has always been that through my love, she came to know God's love. I've done many things in my life that required more self-sacrifice, but somehow this one stands out, possibly because there was no pride or self-interest involved. I think God was pleased with me.

God is pleased and delighted when we become communicators of His love.

The parable Jesus told about the shepherd leaving the ninety-nine sheep for the one lost lamb begins to make sense in this context. So does the old catechism answer I learned by rote as a child: "God made me to know Him, to love Him, to serve Him in this world, and to be happy with Him forever in the next" (*Baltimore Catechism*, p. 1). Only now, as an adult, I see that it is also possible to be happy with Him right now in this world, while carrying the crosses of this life.

God wants us to be happy here and now. And it delights Him to see us help one another. He rejoices with His creatures when they are fully alive. Jesus came that His joy might be ours and that our joy might be complete (Jn 15:11).

Gifted with this insight, as mentioned earlier, I tried a new approach to spirituality. I decided to emphasize the positive side of religion, putting a higher value on pleasing God than I had before. Formerly, I concentrated on avoiding His displeasure; not a bad idea, but one that can get out of hand. Now I began to trust my natural gifts more, like humor, spontaneity and thoughtfulness. I loosened up and developed ways of helping others that flowed more naturally from my personality rather than from any imposed sense of duty. For me this was an unforced, more sincere style of living. It gave me joy because it helped me to feel good about myself. And I began to love God more.

Working one's way from the "feel good" level of faith to the more difficult "Thy will be done" level isn't easy. To my surprise, I found there wasn't that much difference between the two. It seems I had to discover the joy of Christianity before I could make sense out of the cross. Now I find myself coming back to joy no matter what I have to put up with, and I have a better understanding of the words of Jesus: *My yoke is easy and my burden light* (Mt 11:30).

(From R.J., Melbourne, FL)

Eleven years or so ago, my 23-year-old son lay in the hospital facing a second operation in three years for colon cancer. Although, as the doctor put it, he was as healthy as a bull in all other respects, he had only a slim chance of surviving.

While he was the third of five children, his impending death hit me as hard as if he were an only child. I prayed to God, "I do not know Your will. If it is Your will to take him, then take him. But if You have not made up Your mind, then I beg You to spare him. Oh God, I cannot be bitter. I remember the Sullivans who gave up four sailor sons on one navy ship. I remember the

Kennedys who gave up Joe, Jack and Bobby. No, Lord, there is no bitterness in my heart — only resignation to Your divine will."

I think God must have been pleased with me (delighted seems too strong a word. I wonder if any of us can delight Him).

After eight and one-half hours on the operating table, my son was saved. He lives, works and enjoys life today. God knows how I feel: If it is His will He can have everyone and everything I have — He gave it all.

How sweet is the spirit of one who surrenders to the will of God: *If you find your delight in the Lord, He will grant you your heart's desire* (Ps 37).

(From James Ribbe, Nutley, NJ)

When I first read your invitation, I could not think of a single event in my life that qualified as a time I delighted the Lord. Many would come to mind if you were soliciting input for a book entitled, God is Disappointed in You. On reflection, I found this quite sad. However, this reaction is probably not unusual . . . years of conditioning causes one's mind to set toward an ongoing review of sins, not good acts. Well, here goes.

My wife and I, together with our small children, were in a family station wagon on our way to Mass one Sunday morning. It was a wet day and the roadway was slippery. The driver in a car coming my way failed to stop in time and hit a woman as she stepped into the street. I parked, grabbed a blanket and rushed to assure the woman she would be fine. The driver who struck her remained in his car in apparent shock. A police officer arrived and he began dealing with this as though the woman had merely fallen. The driver of the other car remained silent. As the *only witness, I had to convince the officer that he was dealing with a motor-vehicle/pedestrian accident. The woman was eventually taken to the hospital and we all missed Mass. All I could feel that day was guilt for that omission.*

In the weeks that ensued, litigation was initiated between the woman and the driver's insurance carrier. I was called twice to give depositions. In both cases I had to take off from work. The frail woman was slow recovering, but eventually she was compensated out-of-court for her injuries, primarily because of my testimony. Some time after the settlement, her son came by my house with a check for $100 to express his mother's appreciation. I diplomatically declined (though I was tempted), citing that I had simply done my duty.

The most important element of this otherwise quite ordinary story is that our children saw my involvement from start to finish. Today, as young adults, they still remember it. The incident proved to be a practical illustration of Christian responsibility to others — a lesson not available to them as vividly through text books. And God may have delighted in me at least a little bit.

James Ribbe's beautiful story is not unlike the Good Samaritan parable in the Gospel. I'm sure he delighted the Lord that day. But undoubtedly there were many other days, ordinary hum-drum days, in his life when the Lord was delighted with him as well: working hard to support a family, overlooking the faults of others, loving his wife, trying to be a good father. His life was filled with times when he pleased and delighted the Lord, more days than he could ever imagine. It delights the Lord to see us trying to be faithful to our duties in life. He made us for happiness and it pleases Him to admire His success when we live gladly and gratefully.

We put ourselves down too often. Women suffer the most from this negative trait. So many have been made to feel guilty for not being good enough. The tradition which blamed Eve for the fallen condition of the human race has been a constant thorn down through the centuries, and has been unjustly used by many men to keep women under their domination.

To correct this bias, all of us have to go back to the Book of Genesis where we read that after God made the heavens and the earth, the waters, the vegetation, and all the living creatures, He created man and woman in His own image. And He blessed them: *And so it was, God saw all that He had made, and indeed He saw that it was very good* (1:28).

Women are good. Men are good. And all the living creatures on the earth are good. Therefore, I repeat the point: Don't put yourself down! You are made in God's image and likeness. Your dignity as a person is founded upon this truth. You are a holy child of God, and the Father delights in loving you.

> Lord, help me to accept Your love,
> on good days and on bad;
> when I am disappointed with myself,
> and when I'm feeling strong.
> Help me to believe deeply in your unchanging love,
> so that I may always rejoice in it,
> without fear and needless worry.

(From Lida Gall, Crowley, LA)

Your request about God's delight makes me smile and share.

My husband and I are immigrants from the Netherlands and we have twelve children. During World War II, we lived through five years without freedom and even with hunger before we were married. Then there were, of course, days of homesickness, operations and pain; exhaustion was no stranger to us either. Through our faith and trust we know, however, that we can and will survive everything. Don't we all?

Our six daughters and six sons are all married now and we have twelve grandsons and twelve granddaughters up till now! (This is family planning; the Lord did the planning.)

I feel like the flower I put in a vase (a Dutch woman has to have at least one all the time). I love it into life, almost, and I am delighted every time I look at it.

God made me as that flower. He looks at me and is delighted.

Give Him Your Trust

The classic text of Jesus speaking on trust is found in the Gospel of St. Matthew: *My advice is: don't worry about things like food, drink, and clothes. For you already have life and a body — and they are far more important than what to eat and wear. Look at the birds! They don't worry about what to eat — they don't need to sow or reap or store up food — for your heavenly Father feeds them. And you are far more valuable to Him than they are. Will all your worries add a single moment to your life?* (6:25-27).

In Psalm 37 we read, *If you trust in the Lord and do what is good, then you will live in the land and be secure. If you find delight in the Lord, He will grant your heart's desire.*

Accepting the mystery of a love relationship with God is not a pious fantasy. Not at all. It is the central fact of our faith. So the words of Jesus have to be taken seriously. In substance He is saying we worry too much about material things. And He's right.

Fact number one: God is Unchanging Love. We need to develop an unwavering faith in the fact that His love for us is personal. He wants us to trust Him. Granted the experience of His protection may at times elude the senses. Nevertheless, it is real. We have known with certainty for two thousand years that God loves us with an infinite love, but it is surprising how many individual Christians are still learning it for the first time.

(From Alice Dailey, Indianapolis, IN)

Before the advent of wonder drugs, the only known cure for tuberculosis was isolated bed rest. I had just rejoined my good husband and two small girls after a three and one-half year bout with the disease. But even as we rejoiced at the reunion, a new set of problems arose, a possible life-endangering pregnancy. Pressure came from all sides. "Don't dare have any more children. You must live for the two you now have."

What was I to do? Believing deeply in the Church's teaching on birth-control and that God knows best, I placed my trust in Him. Within a year a four-pound, sickly little girl who would need constant care was born. Later a little boy joined us too. Those ensuing years were not easy.

But the God who knows the future foresaw the tragedies that would strike and numb; the untimely deaths of our two older daughters, who were talented young women, and the passing of their father shortly after.

And so, in God's infinite wisdom and compassion He was pleased to send the once "sickly little girl" and her brother who have become my loving, caring mainstays through the years.

Whether you would or could make the decision Alice Dailey made, you have to admit she had courage. She trusted God and lived to be grateful for it.

Sometimes people ridicule us when we go out on a limb for God. Jesus knew that would happen. In His Sermon on the Mount, He said, *Blessed are you when people abuse you and persecute you . . . on My account* (Mt 5:11). It may seem contradictory to speak of happiness in the same breath as risk-taking and even persecution, but countless saints testify to the fact that when they were faithful to the Lord in difficult circumstances, they experienced the deepest joy they had ever known. The gift of joy is beyond our natural understanding, but it grows and grows in proportion to our trust.

Julian of Norwich encouraged us to live gladly no matter what the external circumstances of our life might be, and to do it with the intention of honoring God. Why would anyone engage in such a dream? Because we delight the Lord when we trust Him. And He always rewards our trust with an increase of joy. When we come to the point where we depend on God alone — and not too many reach the state of perfect trust — we are at the height of our human potential.

Jesus assured us that once we truly believe in God's saving love, and act on our belief that He is truly with us at all times, the miseries of this life would no longer disturb us. In the Beatitudes, Jesus instructs us that the troubles of this world count for nothing when seen in the light of the world to come: *Blessed (Happy!) are those who hunger and thirst for justice for they shall be completely satisfied* (Mt 5:6). It is in times of trial that He wants us to remember His love. Trials, therefore, are actually opportunities for spiritual growth. If we see the cross only as a burden, we miss a wonderful chance to grow and to delight the Lord with our trust.

(From Robin A. Kellogg, Baltimore, MD)

I am an adult child of an alcoholic father and a co-dependent mother, neither of whom had a personal relationship with God going for them. So I have had to overcome a lot of internal blocks in my own search for God and struggle to let Him love me and surrender my will to Him.

Being a compulsive person myself by nature, I have a strong tendency to get down on myself for my faults and failure to live up to all I think God wants me to be. I also tend to project my self-dissatisfaction onto Him and I have real trouble letting go of those things in my personality that I cannot change and letting Him control the growth and healing process. It is very difficult for me to believe on a deep level that God loves me as I am right now.

One of the things that is helping to turn this old way of thinking around for me is this book, He and I (Published by Les Editions Paulines, 250 Boul. St. François nord; Sherbrooke, Que. J1E 2B9, Canada). *I have been reading this book at the rate of a few pages a night before I go to bed and finding a real healing power in its message (which is basically the same as yours, that God delights in us personally and not just generally as collective members of His creation, but on a very one-to-one level as distinct individuals with unique gifts that He has purposely planted in us to give Him pleasure).*

Robin Kellogg is referring to a book that I found quite helpful in my own life. It was written by Gabrielle Bossis who was born in Nantes, France in 1874, the youngest child of a family of four children. She was extremely shy as a child but when she grew up she studied nursing. Years later, she discovered a talent for writing and acting. She changed careers, produced her own plays and acted in them, becoming famous throughout France.

On rare occasions in her early life, Gabrielle had been surprised by a mysterious voice from within which she felt with awe, and sometimes with anxious questionings, to be the voice of Christ. She was a prayerful woman all her life, but it wasn't until she was 62 that this mysterious dialogue began to be a regular occurrence. Her spiritual director insisted that she keep a journal. This dialogue continued until her death on

June 9, 1950, and her journal proved to be one of the most astonishing spiritual findings in this century.

Here are some of the earliest excerpts of the Lord speaking to her:

— *1936* —

Be simple with Me just as you are with your own family.
Try to be My smile and My kind voice for everybody.
I'll make your smile a blessing to others.

— *1937* —

Offer Me each moment as it passes . . . then your whole year will be for Me.

In your soul there is a door that leads to the contemplation of God. But you must open it.

My sunsets are also My love. So few of My children look at them to praise Me . . . and yet My love is there.

You are watching the direction in which the train will come. That's the way My eyes are fixed on you, waiting for you to come to Me.

Always be serene and calm. The river reflects the sky, only when it is calm.

Don't say, "Glory to the Father and to the Son," in such a vague way, but wish for this glory in this or that action.

Return good for evil; don't lose a single opportunity.

Don't get the idea that a saint is a saint at every moment, but there is always My grace.

Why do you talk to Me as though I were far away? I am very near, in your heart.

When you are in church get rid of all the thoughts and cares of the day. Just put them aside as you would take off a garment, and be all Mine.

Take the little daily trials with a smile and you will dress My wound.

Be happy when you can offer a little suffering to Me, the suffering One.

Sometimes you feel Me more, sometimes less, but I never change. Don't aim at saying an exact number of wordy prayers. Just love Me simply. A look of your heart. The tender smile of a friend.

Gabrielle Bossis was in touch with God, wouldn't you say? I particularly liked the entry about sunsets being a sign of His love. Other people feel the same way.

(From Edith Paganucci, Ft. Pierce, FL)

Coming back from Chicago in the winter, everything seemed dead. But when we got to Tennessee and it was drizzling and the grass was getting greener and the trees were all blooming, it said to me that God was showing me His love. And when the sun comes out in the morning — going to Mass we see a bright sun shining — I see so much beauty that His beauty alone is something to praise Him with and give Him glory. No matter what our problems are, He speaks to us in the sky, in the ocean waves, the beauty everywhere, to let us know how much He really loves each one of us.

You don't have to be a great saint to know how to be intimate with the Lord. Saints-in-training don't have to seek after joy directly. It comes to them anyway. Joy is the inevitable by-product of a soul surrendered to God. Those who empty themselves for the love of God find all kinds of wonderful gifts waiting for them. Their weakness is turned into strength, and their sorrow into joy.

When Mary, the mother of Jesus, said, *My soul magnifies*

the Lord, my spirit rejoices in God my Savior (Lk 1:46), she was proclaiming the gift of happiness in her own soul. How blessed and fortunate we are to be able to share in the very same gift, which is a reflection of the happiness of God!

St. Thomas Aquinas wrote in his *Summa Theologiae: Happiness is God's above all. . . . For His delight, God has joy in Himself, and in everything else* (1A. 26, 1 & 4). You, my dear friend, are part of that "everything else." God delights in you. Your soul magnifies the Lord when you rejoice in God your Savior. His happiness finds its echo in your own heart.

We were created for happiness, and we are called to live gladly because of the knowledge of God's love. This is the way our heavenly Father, from the beginning, intended us to live. If there were no other reasons for being happy, the fact that our gladness delights the Lord is reason enough to work at dispelling all gloom and doom. By putting away the things that make us sad, like selfishness and sin, we practice the discipline of love. No easy task, I admit, but well worth the effort.

Pray for the grace to trust the Lord. Reach up to God with a childlike trust, and anticipate His loving embrace in return. God delights in a happy soul.

(From Annemarie M. Siegel, Doylestown, PA)

I am now physically handicapped, but in the past I studied ballet.

About two weeks ago I had just returned from a truly grace-filled six-day retreat. It was at a hermitage in New Mexico. In many ways it was the most difficult time of my life, but the fruits of that time were abundant. One of the many graces was the ability to leave my mind behind when I prayed, and just be open to listening and receiving the words and images Jesus wanted to give, instead of my list and agenda.

The last night I found myself dancing down a dusty road singing, 'Zippidy Doo Da,' and Jesus was singing along. When I returned home, after two weeks I still have the clearest image of Jesus coming and dancing with me. This was such a delight and healing. My dream has always been to dance in heaven for the Lord. Jesus showed me that night that, in His eyes, that dream is already true.

Just beneath the surface of every human being there resides the soul of a mystic. You may not feel like one, or even aspire to be one, but I'll bet there have been moments in your life when God's presence was so real you could almost touch Him. These moments may be rare as far as feelings are concerned, but our faith tells us that God is always near. When you trust Him instinctively, the problems that weigh you down become much lighter. Even if your feelings haven't caught up yet, you are in His gentle care. God is preparing you for a share in His glory, even when He sends the cross.

Prayer is difficult for those who are undergoing a time of suffering, and so is trust. The following thoughts may be of help.

(From Elizabeth Burzotta, Marysville, WA)

This will sound awfully simplistic, but I remember a time when I was . . . reading a book on the topic of prayer. The book talked about one of the ways that a person could pray would be just to gaze at the sky. Reading that, I was immediately taken back to a particular time in the past. I was sitting on the steps of Roosevelt High School in my home town of St. Louis. And, as I remembered it, a very peaceful feeling came over me. I gazed up at the sky which was a beautiful blue, with billowing clouds. The weather was warm and comfortable, and the peace I ex-

perienced on the steps of my high school that day long ago, came back to me then and there. I was in total agreement with what I read. Prayer could indeed be just gazing at the sky.

Everything we offer God is His gift to us in the first place. Even our appreciation of a beautiful sunset requires the gift of sight. But trust is of our own creation. Trust is the only thing we have to offer Him that is truly our own. Trust is the love answer, and trust always awakens joy in the soul. *Rejoice in all circumstances, and . . . no matter what happens, always be thankful, for this is the will of God for you who belong to Jesus Christ* (1 Th 5:16-18).

> O Most Trustworthy Father,
> bless me with the gift of confidence
> that I may trust Your love,
> in all circumstances
> all the days of my life.

(From Joseph Hamel, M.D., Minneapolis, MN)

In 1945, while a junior medical student, I assisted my father in the delivery of a baby at St. Mary's Hospital. Last Sunday morning, at 3 a.m., I delivered my last baby.

On my way out of the hospital I stopped in the chapel to utter a prayer of thanksgiving for another healthy baby and for the fact that in these 45 years I had never lost a mother in childbirth.

During my drive home in those wee hours of the morning, I dared to think that I had pleased my God in contributing for these many years to His Mystical Body.

I look forward to retirement in a year and anxiously await my son who is in training at the Mayo Clinic to succeed me in this marvelous profession and family tradition.

CHAPTER SEVEN

Carry His Love To Others

The same Holy Spirit who empowered Jesus to give sight to the blind and hearing to the deaf, abides in you.

Once you open yourself to this idea and understand that God is utterly unselfish and totally sincere, you may begin to trust Him more and live as an instrument of His peace. You will rejoice quietly in the knowledge of His love. Fear will no longer have the same hold over you. You'll be able to let go of anxiety about the past, not perfectly perhaps, but enough to feel more relaxed. You can even begin to get the feeling that God is using your talents to touch the lives and hearts of others in ways you never thought possible.

That has happened in my own life. There are times when I become conscious of God working in me and through me. When that happens, I thank Him and just carry on as though it were the most natural thing in the world. Sometimes, mentally, I just stand on the sidelines and applaud what is happening before my eyes. It's God's doing, not mine.

The idea of being an instrument of the Lord cannot be taken too literally. You are a person, and not a thing to be used like a flute in the hands of a musician. A human being has free will. Human cooperation is needed continually to bring about the full effect of God's action. We tend to underestimate the importance of our own cooperation in the work of grace.

God disposed Himself in such a way as to rely on the free will of Mary to bring about the miracle of the birth of Christ. In order to assume a human nature God needed the cooperation of a woman, and Mary was chosen for some special reason known only to the Trinity.

When God asks any one of us to be His instrument, He is asking us to cooperate with Him so that His divine love will be able to pass through us to others. Quite an honor, and quite a responsibility!

(From Helen LeGrand, Upper Saddle River, NJ)

It was a beautiful autumn day. I decided to forego my usual Saturday routine of cleaning house, shopping, etc., after a busy week at work. There was a day of recollection at St. Elizabeth's College, Convent Station, NJ, so off I went for a restful day of prayer.

During the morning seminar, a woman stood up and started telling her story which was very sad. The facilitator of the group stopped her and said she would see her later, but this was not the time to discuss serious problems. Of course she was right, but the woman sat down and she looked crushed.

As we left the seminar for a break I asked the woman if she would like to sit with me for lunch. She said "Yes." "I guess I made a fool of myself," she said. "No, not at all. Everyone understood, I'm sure. We all have times when we need to talk about our problems." During lunch I listened. She confided to me that she had wanted to commit suicide that morning but she saw the ad for this day of recollection and decided to try it first.

I told her how I handled my problems: one day at a time. How I trusted the Lord to see me through the long haul. We talked all afternoon and then went to Mass together. I prayed for her all day, asking God to give her the grace to go on with life and not to despair. When we parted, she told me she felt renewed.

Several weeks later I met her again, just by chance. She was a different person, smiling, happy, and very grateful to meet me again as she had lost my phone number and wanted to tell me that I had literally saved her life. Many good things had happened to her: she got a new job, met a wonderful man and had reconciled with her son. I was delighted that things had turned out so well for her, and I was so pleased that God let me know the happy ending.

I went to a nearby church to thank God for all His graces and blessings. In the pew there was a prayer booklet. I read these words: "I have seen your compassion for others and you will be blessed for this." Thank you, dear Lord, for blessing my humble efforts to help others.

Human compassion is a beautiful sign of God's love. It is the incarnation of divine compassion. No one should ever feel unworthy of being an instrument, no matter what their past might have been. God is always ready to send new graces to bring about His wonderful plan of salvation.

(From C. Rockwell, Easton, MD)

I made a Cursillo in Chicago in 1979, and since that March weekend, I have realized deeply that the Lord delights in me, and in all of His creation, especially His people. I had my third child in 1981, and I received some insight into the depths of this joy God takes in us when I looked into my baby's face. When I gazed at this tiny infant, drawing life and nourishment from me, I realized at the same time that I draw life and nourishment from my Lord. An infant cannot do anything to please a parent, and yet the simple fact of the baby's presence

*delights even the most crusty bachelors. We can also consider
that infants, at best, are rather noisy and selfish creatures, and
yet we still pour out our love upon them and (sometimes) laugh
at the messes they make, because they are our children.*

A parent will always accept the imperfections of his or her
own children. This simple comparison helps us to see
ourselves from God's perspective.

Moral theology is brimming with references to the ways
we can offend God, but little is ever said of the incredible
power we have to please Him. How an insignificant human
being, a struggling sinner at that, can please the Lord is the
most fascinating part of our religion. You and I were made for
happiness because we are made in the image of Happiness
personified. The very thought of a future united with the source
of all joy brings pleasure to the soul. Our happiness is forever
tied to our degree of union with the All-Holy One.

One of the keys to understanding this mystery is found in
the doctrine of the Eucharist: *Until the Lord comes, therefore,
every time you eat this bread and drink this cup, you proclaim
His death* . . . (1 Cor 11:26). The risen Lord has come to dwell
in you in a tangible way. His power flows through you. Paul
said that Jesus Christ is the same yesterday, today and tomorrow. As He enters the flow of history, His presence — and
therefore God's presence — has an actuality and immediacy
that is real.

To confirm His presence in the world and to affirm it,
Jesus said, *This is My body . . . This is My blood.* He did not
say, "This is My spirit, this is My soul." No, in the reality of the
here and now, in this time and for all time He said, *This is My
body; This is My blood.*

God is not aloof, distant, uninvolved. Jesus is with us
here and now. His passion, death and resurrection are being
lived again in everyone who is animated by His Holy Spirit. It

may be more obvious in some than in others but all of us can be affected in the same way. A woman like Mother Teresa of Calcutta, or a man like the martyred archbishop, Oscar Romero of El Salvador, are two of the more obvious examples of the Lord living in our midst. If you have the eyes to see, and the faith to understand, you will see that you are a holy child of God. The Spirit of Jesus is living in you. You become the hands and the voice of Christ in your particular part of the world. All of God's children who open themselves to the indwelling Spirit become instruments of God's love.

Some may think of this as an extraordinary spiritual experience but, more often than not, it's as mundane as a hospital visit or a committee meeting.

(*From Claire Schutze, Wayne, NJ*)

In March of 1974 I was invited to a priests' meeting at Our Lady of Consolation parish in Wayne. The main thrust of the meeting concerned the thirteen nursing homes in the area and how the priests could accommodate the residents. I had been invited because I had an idea. I remembered my father telling me about the First Saturday Club in Newark and how he helped with the elderly there. I explained the plan and the priests agreed to start up a First Saturday Club in Wayne. Here's the idea: the members of the club are the handicapped and homebound elderly. We gather them together by bus and car and meet in a different host parish on the first Saturday of the month where we have a liturgy at 11:00 a.m. A simple lunch follows, hosted by the ladies of the parish. The purpose of the club is to get the old folks out of their confinement to a more inspiring environment where people pray together and, most important, receive the Holy Eucharist together.

This past September was our 15th anniversary of monthly

meetings. No way could we have done this on our own. God has taken the First Saturday Club as one of His own projects.

When you are there for others, Jesus living in you is also there, and the words of the Father apply to you as well, "This is My beloved one in whom I take delight."

The entire New Testament is overflowing with the Good News about the Father's love for His beloved Son. And we are one with Him! Jesus has empowered us to please the Father. He has given us the gift that all lovers enjoy, the pleasure of giving pleasure.

We give delight and pleasure to God when we allow Him to minister to others through us. Do not let your feelings sabotage your belief in your own power to be a carrier of divine love. Warm, cozy feelings may come to you from time to time, but never consult your feelings to estimate the level of your faith. The absence of good feelings does not indicate a lack of faith. More often than not you will have to ignore your feelings and carry on in dryness and with sheer will power. Faith enables us to do such things.

This is when we need a real sense of the Fatherhood of God. When Jesus said we should call God, "Father," He was not saying that God was a lot like an earthly father. No! What Jesus meant is that God is truly our Father, and our Mother. He delights in His children, and He loves us with a pure love.

You have the power to return the Father's love with a pure heart, not because you are His equal but because you have His Spirit within you. You are a part of the supernatural Love-Force that brings healing to the world. You are part of God's redemptive plan, and He delights in sharing this ongoing creative action with you. He is calling you by name to the fullness of life and joy.

Divine Love is abiding in you. You enter this unspeakable mystery of God's love by virtue of your union with His beloved Son, Jesus Christ. Through Him you participate in God's own life, and become a co-worker with Christ in bringing God's love to the world.

(From Mary Bell Pennock, Elkton, MD)

Eric, my grandson, was born six weeks early in March 1989. He stayed in the hospital for 19 days. I held his tiny body for the first time eight days after he was born. He had all kinds of tubes and machinery helping him breathe. I whispered to him, "I am very happy that you are here in the world. God is helping you to get better, so you can see and run and play with the bunny rabbits in Grandma's yard."

It was important to say something happy to him at this time.

I know God was laughing six months later when Eric and I were on my patio. A bunny rabbit went running by, over near the hedge. I laughed and hugged Eric and thanked God again.

Even if your faith is as tiny as an atom, you should be able to see that there is more to this world than meets the eye. St. Augustine tells us that we *already have the first fruits of the Spirit, and we also have reason for rejoicing, for we are drawing near to the one we love. And not only are we drawing near, we even have some slight feeling and taste of the banquet we shall one day eagerly eat and drink.*

(From P.M., Ocala, FL)

Here is a true story of a time I thought I delighted the Lord.

I was driving into town and I saw this old lady walking along the side of the road. She was about 82. I pulled over and asked her if she would like a ride and she said, "Oh, yes, Honey. I need to go to the store to buy a gift for my new grandson and mail it."

So we continued into town and I went into the store with her and helped her choose a gift, wrapped it for her and took her to the post office and mailed it. Then I took her back home. About three days later, I opened the passenger side of my car and there was $21 lying by the inside of the door. She had lost it and could not get in touch with me. But, thank God, I had her phone number and was able to call her. You can imagine the happiness on this old lady's face when I arrived with the money!

Imagine the happiness on God's face when you do something for Him. He is living in the person you help. We delight the Lord whenever we accept His love and pass it along: *When you did it for the least of My brethren you did it for Me* (Mt 25:40).

Giving and receiving is the way love works. Only those who accept love can fully enjoy its fruits. The same is true of our relationship with God. When His love is accepted and enjoyed it is certain to bear rich fruit, because God's love is efficacious. It always succeeds in accomplishing its purpose: to build up the Kingdom of God and communicate His happiness to all who are disposed to receive it.

A reminder of this is to be found in the popular prayer of St. Francis of Assisi.

> Lord, make me an instrument of your peace,
> where there is hatred, let me sow love,
> where there is injury, pardon,
> where there is doubt, faith,
> where there is despair, hope,
> where there is darkness, light,
> where there is sadness, joy.

Divine Master, grant that I may not so much
seek to be consoled as to console;
to be understood as to understand;
to be loved as to love.
For it is in giving that we receive;
it is in pardoning that we are pardoned;
and it is in dying that we are born to eternal life.
Amen.

(From Mary Fahey, R.N., Brighton, MA)

I try to see God's sufferings in my patients' pain and discomfort, and I try to console them with kind words or just the touch of my hand on their head. Sometimes it's just ordinary things or acts that I do that have extraordinary value. To me, prayer is the most rewarding thing you can do for a patient. The sacredness surrounding death is frightening to a patient. And to try to tell them it is just an open door to heaven to meet our loved ones again is comforting to them in the wee hours of the morning. I think God is pleased with me when I try to bring faith and hope to those in pain.

CHAPTER EIGHT

Take Up Your Cross

Jesus said, *Take up your cross and follow Me* (Mt 16:24). He also said, *If you love Me, keep My commandments* (Jn 14:15). Such statements are not mere suggestions or requests. Jesus demanded that we love one another. *Wherever there is love, there is the cross; and wherever there is the cross, there is a victim* (Dorothy Day).

God's relationship with us is one of love. If any one of us is faced with danger, He will help us. Jesus came to save sinners. His total disregard for personal safety proved the extent of His love. For Jesus, the cross was not only an act of reparation for our sins; it was a public statement, a sign of His passionate love for all of us.

There have been times in your life when loving someone required sacrifices of you. The pain and suffering involved may now be a distant memory, but looking back I'm sure you can say it was worth it. The cross is not always a curse.

Human nature being what it is, however, we cannot expect ourselves to look for crosses. Jesus Himself recoiled from His cross, even though in the end He accepted it.

Saints-in-training often fail to take up their cross. That doesn't make them bad. The French novelist Leon Bloy once said, *The greatest sadness is not to be a saint.* Yes, it is sad. But

I would like to add this joyful note: even as we stumble and fall, by getting up and trying again, we give the Lord great pleasure. He sees every phase of your life, and He knows your good intentions.

The Lord is like a great artist painting a magnificent portrait of you. At any given moment you may not recognize yourself; the saint within is not visible. You won't see yourself as radiant and noble. In fact, in the beginning the painting may appear to be grotesque. But as the Lord progresses, your face will become more beautiful, your smile more glorious.

God works in secret. Only He knows what your final portrait will look like. Perhaps this explains so much of the confusion we experience in life. The identity crises so many people go through are part of their growth process.

Each day we find out a little more about ourselves. We are torn between two desires: one keeping us chained to selfishness, and the other helping us to reach up to God in self-surrender.

God's skill in making saints out of ordinary people cannot be doubted. Trusting Him can be a cross at times, but this cross is good.

Here is a letter from someone who knows how to carry her cross joyfully.

(From Leticia G. Caceres, Boston, MA)

While I was still in my native country, The Philippines, I learned this song:

Ang Buhay Nang Kristiano	*The life of a Christian*
Ay Masayang Tunay	*is truly a happy one*
Masayang Tunay	*truly a happy one*
Masayang Tunay	*truly a happy one*
Masayang Tunay	*truly a happy one*

Wherever I am, I love to sing this song, especially after praying and elevating to God all my aches and pains and trials and tribulations of daily living. When there are people around, I just sing this song in my mind. People have actually asked me why I always seem so happy and enthusiastic about everything. My secret, of course, is that I go on with my daily activities with a song in my heart.

The cross and the spirit of joy are not incompatible. Even if you are suffering unendurable pain or misery, even if you are the victim of malice as Jesus was, the knowledge of God's love can be a source of comfort, strength and joy.

All of the suffering and misery in the world cannot blot out or even diminish God's unchanging love. Suffering can be understood within a larger context than the pain of the present moment. Suffering can become so severe that all rationality seems to disappear, and good people find themselves doubting God's love. St. John the Baptist, whom Jesus called the greatest man born of woman, doubted when he was imprisoned by Herod. Don't be surprised if you have dark thoughts about suffering. "Why me? Why this? Why now?" Such thoughts are almost to be expected.

Try to keep in mind the fact that God and you have the same goal: to help you find happiness for all eternity. Achieving that goal requires a gradual death to the things of this world. You may never fully understand it, but there it is.

Some people believe that God doesn't care about them. If He did, they muse, why all this misery? The fact is that He always cares. In spite of all the trials that we have to face in life, we must continue to trust His love.

No one can fathom the mystery of suffering, why good people are so often the ones who suffer the most. All we can do is accept the mystery. *God grant me the serenity to accept the things I cannot change, the courage to change the things I can, and the wisdom to know the difference* (Serenity Prayer).

Thousands of personal letters come to me each year at the Christophers. They come from people all over the world. Many of these good people are carrying heavy crosses. Let me mention some of the ones I read this morning as I prepared for Mass.

Please pray for my son. He's 27 and on drugs.

Pray for J.D. He has a spot on his lung; wife is blind; son, mentally retarded.

Please pray for B. so she will not live anymore with the man who beats her.

Please pray for my knees; I'm in great pain walking. Also, pray for my mother's Parkinson's disease.

My husband and I have a child, M., 9 years old with Fragile X syndrome (a rare genetic condition that involves low muscle tone and mental retardation) so I'd appreciate any prayers that can come from you.

I have a throat irritation that causes my food to stick. Specialists have examined me, but so far no cure. So would you please light a candle for me.

Please pray to save R's marriage.

My heart goes out to each of them and I add my own intentions: sick members of my family, my co-workers, people I know who are suffering in confusion, doubt and pain. All I can think of is God's heart. If one as limited as myself can feel deeply for these good people, how much more does the Lord, who knows all their needs, before we even ask Him for His help?

Behind all our pain there is a reason. And God knows the reason. Sometimes it may be obvious, sometimes it is hidden, but most of us have to admit that adversity has often brought out the best in us. We simply have to keep searching for understanding to discover who we really are and what role the Lord has assigned to us in life.

The following is a favorite text of mine.

I asked God for strength that I might achieve,
I was made weak that I might learn humbly to obey.
I asked for health that I might do great things,
I was given infirmity that I might do better things.
I asked for riches that I might be happy,
I was given poverty that I might be wise.
I asked for power that I might have the praise of men,
I was given weakness that I might feel the need of God.
I asked for all things that I might enjoy life,
I was given life that I might enjoy all things.
I got nothing that I asked for, but everything I had hoped for.
Almost despite myself, my unspoken prayers were answered.
I am, among all men, most richly blessed.

(An Unknown Confederate Soldier)

There are times when we simply do not understand life. We panic. We act foolishly. We wait for someone to explain what life is all about. At times we're aggravated by our own failure to understand it all. At times we may even be angry with God. But for the faithful Christian, one theme remains true: God is unchanging love.

(From Rosa Baines, Edmonton, Canada)

I have at times wondered whether God allows sorrow and pain in our lives so that we can truly appreciate the times of happiness and joy . . . a sunrise or sunset, birds soaring, flowers blooming, celebrating Christmas with family and friends, attending weddings or baptisms, watching children play. . . .

We really do not know the why and wherefore of pain. Theologically it is explained as the result of original sin. But for many, that idea only opens up new questions. What we do know is that God is in the heavens. He sent His only begotten Son to convey a message of hope to us, to tell us to live joyfully, and to anticipate eternal happiness.

How delighted God is when we believe in His love through all the storms of life. Our crosses serve many purposes which we rarely see at the time of suffering. Often the cross brings us closer to God through a spiritual bonding born of need. We rise to heroism, and find strengths we never knew we had. We edify others, win them graces through our prayers, and purify our own souls. Even before we experience the joys of heaven, there is joy in the knowledge that God is loving us all along the way.

Try not to let pain darken your spirit. It may at times; you're only human. But don't be too discouraged. Suffering is not a sign of God's disfavor, and it can always be used for a good purpose. If you can find relief from the pain through medical help, do it, by all means. But if you can't, try to accept it willingly and lovingly for whatever good God can make of it when offered to Him. You may never know how much good you are doing, but one day it will be revealed to you.

In heaven the scales of justice will be balanced. Leave it at that and carry your cross with courage. You may not understand God's silence, but never mistake it for His absence. His love is always with you.

(From B. Christopher, IL)

My father died in a state hospital from the 3rd stage of syphilis when I had just turned seventeen. I married my wife when I was twenty seven and we ended up with eleven children, four boys and seven girls, all within fifteen years. Through the course of our marriage of forty two years, in the last twenty years, six of the eleven children have been stricken with mental illness: five with manic-depression, one with schizophrenia. I think I myself am a manic depressive, but with faith and God's grace I have somehow managed to keep a steady course for our family (towards where, only the Lord knows).

There have been so many experiences in our lives that I feel I could write a book. Our God is not only a God of joy and happiness, but a God of compassion, consolation, mercy and love.

The miracle is that my wife and I and our family are still on the same path Christ put us on and that we ourselves haven't as yet "gone bananas."

Not everyone could be as brave as this man. His spirit of childlike faith, without a trace of bitterness, is an inspiration to me. I see a saint-well-along-the-way in his gentle humor.

Carrying the cross isn't easy. St. Paul pleads with us to carry our cross with courage: *I have told you often — and I repeat it today with tears in my eyes — that there are many who are behaving as enemies of the cross of Christ. . . . For us, our homeland is heaven, and from heaven comes the Savior we are waiting for, the Lord Jesus Christ. He will transfigure these wretched bodies of ours into copies of His glorious body, and He will do this by the same power He has to subdue the entire universe* (Ph 3:18-21).

The power of prayer works wonders for the drooping spirit. St. Francis de Sales once said, "Don't be discouraged because you're discouraged."

It's normal to want to run away from the cross. Don't be surprised if you're not up to carrying it. But how pleased the Lord is with someone who prays for the grace to grin and bear it! Even if they cry alone, or tearfully accept the consolation of friends and relatives who can do little more than stroke their brow, their time of suffering can win rich rewards for themselves and for those they love. The cross is good.

(From Katherine Karras, Hudson, WI)

It was a hot September morning. I was carrying my sixth child. My legs were swollen. I was BIG and tired of waiting. I was 46 years old and the mother of five other children. Would He send me enough strength and energy to take care of this baby? I was determined to do everything I could to help this child into the world, so I trudged my way up the church steps forcing myself to go to confession. I stopped to catch my breath and looked up at the altar. Just as my fingers touched the holy water, a delightful fragrance enveloped me. It seemed to be coming from the altar. I tried to kneel but the sweet fragrance held my attention. There was no one in the church. I went into the confessional and briefly confessed my sins. After the priest gave me absolution, I said, "Father, did the sisters spray the altar? There's such a wonderful fragrance in the church."

There was a long silence, then the priest said, "When did you notice it?" I stated it was when I touched the holy water. He gave me a blessing and I knelt at the last kneeling bench to say my penance. The lovely fragrance was all around me. Somehow I got down the church steps. It was more like floating. The fragrance faded but the memory of that special time, when God's angels must have been near, is still fresh.

Oh yes, we had an 8 lb. 13 oz. baby girl whom we named Mary. She has been such a blessing. She's married now with two children, a good husband, and she's in her fourth year of college. Me? I'm still going strong, teaching in a small college part-time, loving my family, 14 grandchildren, and loving my students.

How wonderful it would be if we could all receive such a marvelous answer to our prayers, reminding us of God's sweet love. Maybe we would learn to bear our infirmities with more patience. But alas, most of us have to plug along with blind faith.

Those who turn to the Lord in difficult times, delight Him. He wants to share the cross with you. He wants to become your Simon of Cyrene, only His service is freely given. Dispose your soul for an increase of grace because every gesture of love you offer the Lord is answered with a lavish outpouring of His graces. He can never be out-done in generosity.

My dear people, don't be bewildered or surprised that you should be tested by fire. There is nothing extraordinary in what has happened to you. If you can have some share in the sufferings of Christ, be glad, because you will enjoy a much greater gladness when His glory is revealed. It is a blessing for you when they insult you for bearing the name of Christ, because it means that you have the Spirit of glory, the Spirit of God resting upon you (1 Peter 4:12-15).

Father, help me to understand this mystery.
Teach me how to accept my pain with courage,
even as I seek healing and relief.
I offer all my sufferings and humiliations
in a spirit of reparation, and with the help of your grace.
I promise perfect obedience and perfect love. Amen.

(From Jo Stonitsch, Crystal River, FL)

I am almost 75 years old, and most certainly have experienced many delights from God. Though we saw tragedy in our son's accidental death by electrocution a few years ago, and the so-recent mental illness of my husband, whereby I have had to place him in a nursing home, I know that God still delights in me.

I spend many hours alone. However, I call these hours purification times, times I become solely His. . . . He talks with me, and I with Him . . . silent whisperings of enjoyment knowing that I am never alone . . . that He delights in my aloneness. He soothes my anxieties, makes me feel useful, shows me love through my children, grandchildren, my sisters and friends.

He lets me see:

> The morning sun closer and bigger,
> The trees greener and taller,
> The birds more colorful and flightier,
> The squirrels more playful and faster,
> The flowers prettier,
> The children happier,
> The moon brighter,
> The stars shinier. . . .
> And then, I see God smiling at me.
> I know that He is my delight and I am His.

CHAPTER NINE

Cultivate Holy Desires

Ask and you will be given what you ask for. Seek and you will find. Knock and the door will be opened. For everyone who asks, receives. Anyone who seeks will find. If only you will knock, the door will be opened (Mt 7:7-8).

It is said that your treasure is in the desires of your heart. *The entire life of a good Christian is in fact an exercise of holy desire. You do not yet see what you long for, but the very act of desiring prepares you so that when He comes, you may see and be utterly satisfied* (St. Augustine).

What does St. Augustine mean by the phrase, *the act of desiring prepares you?* I think his words can be taken on face value. For instance, when you smell food cooking on a hot stove, your appetite comes alive. You want to sample the delicious treat being conjured up before your eyes. In the same way, God prepares your heart for the great divine encounter that takes place in heaven.

If you develop a taste for God now, and allow it to grow into a flaming desire, your soul will expand and magnify your love. God is aware of every movement in your heart. In fact, He leads you to new heights precisely through your own desires.

Since all holy desires are a gift from God in the first place, it's good to realize that He is constantly drawing you closer to

Him by a subtle attraction that never tampers with your
freedom.

(From F.S., no address)

*After many years of almost daily attendance (I'm now 77
years old) at the Holy Sacrifice of the Mass, I have this feeling of
God's delight when during Mass I say this prayer: "Be pleased
with me, O Heavenly Father, as I desire to offer you a holy
sacrifice, a pure sacrifice, and a pleasing sacrifice, through the
hands of Your Son, our Lord Jesus Christ, for the salvation of the
faithful and all sinners."*

Be pleased with me . . . as I desire to offer you a holy
sacrifice. What a lovely thought!

The desire to please the Lord is in itself pleasing to Him.
A holy desire is a sign of God's presence. The good Lord
created us to share His happiness for all eternity, and He wants
us to begin right now. That means you have the power to please
Almighty God continually not only by your actions, but by your
good intentions and your holy desires.

When you feel a longing for God stirring within your soul,
encourage it. The heart has its own language: *For we don't even
know what we should pray for, nor how to pray as we should.
But the Holy Spirit prays for us with such feeling that it cannot
be expressed in words. And the Father, who knows all hearts,
knows that the Spirit prays for us in harmony with God's own
will. Thus we know that all that happens to us is working for our
good if we love God and are fitting into His plans* (Rm 8:26-28).

We penetrate the mystery of God's love, not through the
mind, but through the language of the heart.

May I share one of my own desires with you: I want to
please God as often as possible. Even though I'm far from

where I would like to be in the spiritual life, I feel a desire to be better, more faithful to God than I have been in the past. I see this desire as a precious gift. I don't let the negative feelings take over. I take the approach that the Lord is pleased with me even though I'm not always pleased with myself. It may sound like a contradiction, but I think of life as a time of learning. Like a child learning to ride a bicycle with his father at his side, I know I please my Father by my effort to keep trying.

I find myself more eager to please the Lord than I used to be. I may go out of my way to help someone when I feel like staying home and minding my own business, and whisper as I do it, "This one's for you, Lord." This is not to say that the person I contact is simply being used. I am motivated by love and concern. But when I'm too lazy to act on my own good intentions, I often get the push I need by looking into the eyes of God and saying, "I hope this pleases You." I can sense Him smiling back at me.

While speaking of my own spiritual growth, don't think that I'm boasting. I know everything is a gift and, like St. Paul, I only boast of my weakness: *I don't understand myself at all. The good that I would do, I do not, and that which I would not do, that I do* (Rm 7:15).

Desires of the heart are like seeds that grow into full-blown trees. In the beginning they do not have great power, but they grow and their progression is inevitable. This is true both for holy desires and for unholy desires to which we give our consent.

When you are tempted, never say, "God sent me this temptation." God does not tempt us to do anything wrong. *Everyone who is tempted is attracted and seduced by his own wrong desires. Then the desire conceives and gives birth to sin. And when sin is fully grown, it too has a child. And that child is death* (Jm 1:12-18).

We are all capable of sin if we allow our desires to drift in the wrong direction. But if we commit ourselves to pleasing God, the strength of the Lord empowers us to steer ourselves in the right direction. Holy desires are gifts of love from God. Cherish them and use them to transform the dark corners of your soul into areas of light.

(From Thomas Downey, Philadelphia, PA)

First of all, it's beyond my comprehension that God can delight in the likes of me. But I'm sure He does. The one quality of my life I think the Lord most delights in is my perseverance. I had a very unhappy childhood. To top it off, I lost my Dad as a small boy. I guess I was looking for love and attention. I became a real hell-raiser both in public and then in Catholic schools. College students rebelled in the 60's; I went on strike in the 30's.

I always wanted to be an altar boy. The good nuns were horrified at the idea. After trying for over three years, I caught the nun off guard and said, "If I reform, could I be an altar boy?" Well, she gave me a trial and I reformed overnight. My whole personality changed, e.g., I served more Masses in two years than other boys did in four or five. I volunteered for the 6:00 a.m. Mass every day during the summer months. I won every honor an altar boy could win. Most of all God gave me a strong love of daily Mass and the Eucharist.

Later, as an adult I served Mass whenever I could in this country and in the South Pacific for over 50 years. The Lord saved my life during the war; I was a hair away from death. In thanksgiving, I promised Him I would work for my parish and Church. I've been doing that for over 43 years, a lector for over 25 years and a Eucharistic minister for nine. I work with the parish sick and shut-ins; I've been involved with our prayer group for 12 years. I'm Deputy Captain of a weekend retreat at Malvern for 42 years. I've been involved with the Knights of Columbus and community work for over 35 years.

I am now retired and work as a volunteer with the Holy Redeemer Hospice program with terminal cancer and AIDS patients.

If I lived a thousand years, I could never thank our God for all He has done for me. I would say my perseverance in becoming an altar boy had to be His biggest delight.

Isn't it amazing what a strong desire can do to change a person's life around? What about your desires? Have you ever thought about becoming a saint? Why not? All you need is faith and a little imagination.

* * *

I'd like to tell you another personal story about one of my holy desires. It came about because of something St. Peter did nearly 2000 years ago.

To offset his threefold denial of our Lord, Jesus asked St. Peter to make a threefold profession of his love: *"Do you love Me?" "Yes, Lord, You know that I love You."* But the Lord wanted more than words. *"Then feed My lambs."* Three times He asked, *"Do you love Me?"* And three times Peter replied, *"Yes, Lord, You know that I love You."* Each time, Jesus repeated His request, *"Then feed My lambs."* The last time, after the third profession of love, the Lord said, *"Feed My little sheep"* (Jn 21:17).

I mention the words of Jesus to Peter again because they have been highly influential in my own life. In the years when I was struggling with my vocation, I didn't feel strong enough or worthy enough to undertake the responsibilities of the priesthood. For some five or six years I pretended to myself that the stirring in my heart about becoming a priest was a pious illusion, not a real calling.

I decided not to desire the priesthood, and gave myself

full permission to dream about a happy marriage and a successful career. As I worked toward this goal, getting my degree
from Fordham in Business Administration and going on lots of
dates, I kept praying for God's help because my internal
confusion and doubt would not go away. I kept getting a
message: "Follow Me!" It was so overpowering that even the
normal drives of youth could not compete with it. I couldn't
pretend any longer. I knew God wanted something more from
me. I really hoped it wasn't true, but I sensed that He wanted
me to be a priest. As much as I tried to deny it, I couldn't get rid
of the idea.

After college I was drafted into the Army. The Korean
War was winding down, but the draft was still going strong. I
went through basic training and ended up as an M.P. at Fort
Sam Houston, San Antonio, Texas, in the 62nd Platoon which
was the Military Police Honor Guard for what was then the
Fourth Army Headquarters. About a year passed when the
Post Chaplain, Father (Major) George Phillips, a good and holy
priest from the Diocese of Ogdensburg, NY, invited me to be
his assistant. He saw me at Mass and communion nearly every
day (I was praying for the grace of a happy marriage, believe it
or not). Thoughts of the priesthood persisted in all of that, so I
was thrilled with the idea of working as a Chaplain's Assistant.
Once I began I soon realized that I was happier than I had been
in years. I loved the day-to-day routine of working around the
chapel. It was during that year that I finally took the dreaded
leap into the dark and said "Yes" to God.

It was a tremendous relief. At last I found the focus I
needed in my life, and I began to cultivate the desire to be a
priest. I began dreaming of one day offering holy Mass.

During my years in the seminary, I was sustained through
long, lonely winters by this strong desire which I know was a
gift from God. I remember how deeply I felt about it. If I could
offer only one Mass in my entire life, I believed the whole

seminary ordeal would have been worth it. The Mass is a communal banquet as well as a memorial of the death of Jesus on the cross. It unites the people of God who are all part of the Mystical Body of Christ, people from all corners of the world.

This one desire gave birth to many others. I accepted the words of Jesus, *Feed my lambs*, as a personal command. They awakened in me a strong desire to do exactly as He asked. I was given the grace to want what God wanted, and to love what He loved as I prepared myself for a life of service to the Gospel of Jesus. All of this helps me to explain the power of one holy desire as a motivator and a catalyst. Such longings of the heart also give an inner joy that this world cannot give.

(From Mary Nester, Harrisburg, PA)

Last fall our garden gave us enough pumpkins to decorate with and to have for pies. But also last fall our son's band organization sold pies for a fund raiser. Because we wanted to support the band group, we decided to buy our Thanksgiving pies from him. Yet I still wanted to use our pumpkins, so I called our city's Bethesda Mission. Sure enough, they needed pies. So that afternoon my husband and I delivered warm, fresh pumpkin pies to the Mission. I truly believe that the secretary's smile and "Thank you" to us reflected God's delight.

It's far easier to love God when you know He is smiling down upon you. If you fear His punishment all the time you miss the sunshine of His love. But what about the harsh words of Jesus in the Gospels? What about the fear He inspired? *Because you are lukewarm, I vomit you out of my mouth* (Rv 3:16).

I remember being taught over and again how God would punish me if I was bad. During my childhood, the whole

Catholic mystique was saturated with thoughts of hell and eternal punishment. Many Catholics fell away from the faith because of this heavy emphasis on the negative. Father Raymond Brown, the Scripture scholar, writes, "The number of people who have turned away from the Church because they found it too forgiving is infinitesimal; the number who have turned away because they found it unforgiving is legion." The spiritual life back then was fraught with fear. Every step spelled danger, and the possibility of making a mistake was a constant preoccupation. There was little room in such a gloomy scenario for appreciating the smile of God.

I came to an appreciation of God's smile quite late in life. Of course, I had a vague idea that we could please or displease Him. But I never thought much about how I could please Him personally. I had a cognitive knowledge of His love, but no appreciative knowledge. I thought mainly of my duties, not of my privileges as a child of God.

Sacred Scripture told us of God's love, but I saw this against a backdrop of fear. In itself, a little fear may be a good thing. The Book of Proverbs calls it the beginning of wisdom. But fear is only the *beginning* of wisdom. Mature wisdom no longer dwells on fear. We need balance in order to become healthy and holy people.

Today, I try to live in a childlike spirit, honoring God's love with my joy, being happy with Him as much as is humanly possible for me. Lots of times I revert back to my former ways and let fear take over, but I fight back and the attacks are mild and short-lived. The more I look for ways to delight the Lord, the easier I find it to be free of needless worry. To explain this more clearly I'd like to share another personal story with you.

About six or seven years ago, I started experiencing a strange buzzing in my ears. It gradually became quite shrill and annoying. Since the noise was constant, I began going to doctors and specialists, and soon found out the condition is known as *tinnitus*. It's quite common, and it drives people up the wall. There is no cure for it.

So there I was with the rest of the tinnitus-sufferers, trying to do my best to adjust to a most unpleasant high-pitched whistle sounding in my head morning, noon and night. It's like listening to air being released from a tire valve for the rest of your life. To cope with it, I decided to put my new found attitude to work on the problem. In desiring to please the Lord in all circumstances, I began to pretend my noises were, themselves, not a problem but a hymn of the universe, the sound of winds blowing in outer space, or the song of angels offering their thanksgiving to God. Far-fetched, I admit, but it's surprising how comforting the thought was. Now, when the noises become annoying, I just imagine they are my unceasing prayer of praise and I smile.

St. Paul urged us to pray without ceasing. With tinnitus, there are no distractions. It just goes on and on. I now have a built-in system for unceasing prayer. And you know what? The noises don't bother me the way they did. I even forget about them most of the time, except when I consciously offer them as my prayer of praise.

I have to laugh at how frantic I was about the condition in the beginning. Don't get me wrong. I wouldn't wish tinnitus on anybody, but I've come to think of it as a blessing in my life. My desire to make the Lord smile has paid off in peace of soul and mind.

Since I know God loves me most tenderly, I honor His love with a joyful heart, and nothing is going to take that from me. I have taken responsibility for maintaining my own happiness in good season and bad. With the help of God's grace I will never allow anything to poison the delicious joy I feel deep within me. Beneath the sound of a thousand crickets chirping in my ear, I have a sweet peace in the knowledge that my offering is pleasing to the Lord. In fact, I have a kind of audacious knowledge that it delights Him.

There are many other ways to delight the Lord, but loving one's neighbor is the surest way.

(From Clementina Auciello, Brighton, MA)

As a hospital volunteer, I try to help the sick. I remind them to pray, give them a glass of water, feed them, wipe their brows and sing a hymn to the Lord and His Blessed Mother with them. I think maybe the most humble thing I do is cut and clean their finger nails. When I do all these things for the sick, I see the face of God in them. In helping them, I help myself. It makes me happy and gives my life meaning too. I think I delight the Lord when I help the sick.

If you desire to delight the Lord, you will succeed. Let me tell you how a few of the saints managed their lives.

St. Therese of Lisieux, mentioned earlier, was born in France in 1873. While still a teenager she entered a Carmelite monastery where she lived a contemplative life. She often dreamed of becoming a martyr, heroically giving her life to God in a faraway land. This excerpt from her autobiography tells us about her holy desire.

Since my longing for martyrdom was powerful and unsettling . . . I persevered in reading and did not let my mind wander until I found this encouraging theme: "Set your desires on the greater gifts. And I will show you the way that surpasses all others." For the Apostle (St. Paul) insists that the greater gifts are nothing at all without love and that the same love is surely the best path leading directly to God. At length I had found peace of mind. Love appeared to me to be the hinge for my vocation. Indeed . . . I saw that love is everything, that this same love embraces every time and every place. In one word, love is everlasting.

In this connection, Therese prayed that her love would reach the ends of the earth. She dreamed of being a foreign missionary and prayed for priests all over the world. She died on September 30, 1897, and in 1925 Pope Pius XI made her a saint of the Church. Today she is the patron saint of foreign missions.

How a young woman, leading a hidden life in France and dying at the age of 24, could become the modern heroine of missionaries is not for me to explain, except to say that the Holy Spirit brings to fulfillment the dreams He inspires. Let your dreams and desires soar to heaven. Have confidence that the Lord, who inspires all holy dreams, will make your dreams come true. Wonderful things will happen in your life.

Another great saint worth studying is St. Ignatius of Loyola. He was born in 1491 at Loyola, Spain. He spent his early years as a soldier, and was wounded in battle. While recuperating, he used to read a great deal and daydream for hours afterward. He imagined himself doing spectacular things for God, deeds more dramatic than those of St. Francis of Assisi. The following excerpt is taken from the life of St. Ignatius by Luis Gonzalez.

When Ignatius reflected on worldly thoughts, he felt intense pleasure; but when he gave them up out of weariness, he felt dry and depressed. Yet when he thought of living the rigorous sort of life he knew the saints had lived, he not only experienced pleasure when he actually thought about it, but even after he dismissed these thoughts he still experienced great joy. . . . Then he understood his experience: thoughts of one kind left him sad; the others, full of joy.

Later, when he became a priest, he encouraged his Jesuit students to engage in mental exercises to quicken their desire for a holy life. He was also a man of joy, remembering the words of St. Francis of Assisi, "Leave sadness to the devil. The devil has reason to be sad."

Ignatian teachings on meditation are part of the rich legacy of his spirituality, which always aims at loving God and giving Him honor and glory. St. Ignatius pleased the Father with his passionate idealism. We would do well to imitate him.

Another great saint, also mentioned earlier, is St. Teresa of Avila. She was born in Avila, Spain in 1515 and died in Alba in 1582. Like St. Therese of Lisieux, she, too, was a Carmelite who enjoyed private revelations from God. When she attempted to reform her order, she met with much resistance, but she persevered with undaunted determination. In training her novices, she always insisted on the importance of fostering holy desires.

She trained the young nuns to develop an inner freedom that would break through any barriers that held them back from loving God wholeheartedly. *Imagine yourself*, she would say, *serving the Lord with great courage, because His Majesty loves courageous and daring souls.* Here was a holy desire planted in the minds of her little ones. She knew with certainty that God reacts with delight not only to our feats of daring, but also to our holy dreams and desires. Fostering holy desires and imaginations is the purpose behind the practice of daily meditation.

Once again, I make the point: accepting the mystery of God's love consists not in abandoning fact for fiction, but in embracing a truth hidden from the learned and clever, a truth revealed only to those who open their hearts to God.

Holy desires should be encouraged, even if they are larger than life. I'll share another dream of mine with you.

One day I would like to see a dedicated group of television professionals form a company to produce high quality TV spots and TV specials aimed at winning the hearts and minds of viewers to the person and the message of Jesus Christ. They should develop a strategic plan to show the Catholic Church in its best light. The validity of the Church as an instrument of God's grace is seen only by those with real faith. So many of the external trimmings of the Church distort its inner beauty.

I see this group as a spiritually motivated team contributing their time and talents, not for monetary gain, but for the love of God. Someday, I hope some gifted lay person will take the initiative to find a way to make this dream come true.

Too many people in today's world see the Church as a pompous institution run by pompous men. They miss the holiness that keeps it all together. What people need to see is the honesty, sincerity, straightforwardness, and the signs of genuine compassion that abound in the Church, the very virtues Jesus praised in the Gospel. We need to find the noble elements of the Church and showcase them.

A good tree produces good fruit. A bad tree never produces good fruit. If we can show real holiness, people will be attracted to the source of it, Jesus Christ. Jesus can be found in the Eucharist, in the Scriptures, and in the People of God, the Church, the Mystical Body of Christ.

A small group of talented professionals could produce memorable TV productions, and perhaps even movies that would make our faith come to life. Millions of people all over the world would benefit from such dedication.

Maybe my dream will come true someday after I'm gone from the scene. I pray that it will. If my bishop gives me permission, I might even start it off myself. But he may have other plans for me. Holy dreams are only holy when they are under the control of the Holy Spirit, so I defer to my superiors in these matters. Even so, I know the Lord will light a spark in someone's heart and one day that spark will burst into a great flame giving light to the world. When that happens the Lord

will be exceedingly pleased, and my cup of joy will be filled to
overflowing.

> Cry out with joy to the Lord, all the earth.
> Serve the Lord with gladness.
> Come before Him singing for joy.
> Know that He, the Lord, is God.
> He made us, we belong to Him,
> We are His people, the sheep of His flock.

(Psalm 100)

(From S.M., a teenager, Boston, MA)

If delight means to please, I think God was delighted last week when I was on a long bus trip. We travelled five days and a lady, 85 years old, wanted to sit in the seat where I was. I offered her the window position and found out she was stone deaf, without a hearing aid. I became her ears for the entire trip, looking straight at her as I mouthed words to her about the changes in schedule or the countryside.

I helped her on and off the bus. I found her a table in the dining room, guided her into the restaurants and buildings, etc. She was very thankful, and she seemed to have an all-round delightful time.

CHAPTER TEN

Pray With An Unwavering Faith

Q. So you're saying that holy desires are a gift from God, and that they transform the soul, and that we have the power to delight the Lord not only with our deeds but also with our desires?

A. Exactly.

Q. Then how does prayer fit into this?

A. Prayer is the expression of our desire. Prayer is the outpouring of our faith, and God is pleased with an authentic faith which is free of doubt. His love is unchanging and unconditional. That means a believer can have certainty about it. But this is not a wide-eyed belief in some vague divine insurance policy. Christian faith is firm in the knowledge that our relationship with God is personal, and the things Jesus promised are true and "will come to pass."

Jesus is the basis of our faith and He is the reason for our certainty. He is also the object of our faith. Through Him we come to know the Father.

Not only does Jesus give us new knowledge about God. He assures us that if we abide in Him, He will empower us to carry His Spirit into the world so that wonderful things will begin to happen. *Truly, truly I say to you, he who believes in me will perform the same works as I do Myself. He will perform even greater works because I am going to the Father. Whatever you*

*ask for in My name I will do, so that the Father may be glorified
in the Son. If you ask anything in my name I will do it* (Jn
14:12-15). Please notice, Jesus promises action: *I will do it!*
Because He made such a definite promise you can be sure He
is delighted when you take Him at His word.

**Q. Yes, but what about the times He is silent? Most of the
time God seems so remote.**

A. Don't mistake God's silence as a sign of His absence.
The Lord taught us to say: "Thy will be done." Maybe your
faith has been too weak to interpret God's silence properly.

Often God wants to give us something but He sees our
soul is not ready for it. He stretches us by waiting, allowing our
own longing to expand our capacity to receive Him. Remember, His grace is given in proportion to our desire. He
expects us to be diligent in asking for what we need.

Some of the greatest breakthroughs in spiritual growth
come about during times of crisis when we learn what we're
made of in the face of adversity. God doesn't abandon us. He
simply lets us learn to swim at times on our own. Grace builds
on nature, and God wants us to increase our desire for Him
before He satisfies us.

Q. Please expand on that idea.

A. Jesus never spoils His children. He challenges them
to become more holy. In the Epistle of St. James (1:5-6) we
read: *If anyone lacks wisdom, let him ask God who gives to all
men liberally . . . but let him ask in faith, not wavering, for he
who wavers (doubts) is like a wave in the sea, driven and tossed
by the wind.*

Q. Can you teach me how to pray?

A. Abbot John Chapman once wrote, "The only way to
pray well is to pray often." I'm not going to improve on that.
Think about God more, and ask His help more. There is a door
that leads to God within your own heart, but you must open it.

He is always there waiting for you to come to Him. Do not try to force feelings of any kind. No matter what you may be feeling at any given moment, go to Him and offer yourself to Him just as you are.

True prayer is in the will. It is the will to give yourself to God that counts. If you're feeling sad on a particular day, call on the Lord in your misery. Ask Him to be your strength and your joy. Offer Him your bad feelings. And, if that's the best you can do, be at peace. Don't expect emotional relief right away. It will come, but be patient. Accept yourself as human and ask for His help to be more holy. Ask with the confidence of a child in the arms of a loving Father.

If you're in doubt about any of this, don't worry. Ask Him to supply you with greater wisdom. Believe that He cares and carry on. Draw from Him, absorb His love. It delights Him to feed you. God delights in all your holy thoughts and desires, so try not to sabotage yourself, fretting over everything that crosses your mind. If you always listen to your fears you'll only become morose and miss some wonderful opportunities to delight the Lord.

Q. How can I make myself believe with an unwavering faith?

A. Faith is a gift, but it's a gift that you can have if you really want it. You can't make yourself believe, but you can pray for an increase of faith, and God will favor your request. Pray without giving up and you will eventually draw down graces which illuminate your mind, giving you a new surge of holy energy. By the power of the Word of God and the Indwelling Holy Spirit you will be transformed into a true believer. St. Paul described the end result when he said, *I live, not I, but Christ lives in me* (Gal 2:20).

Just do your best not to waver even if your feelings haven't caught up yet. The very desire to believe deeply is already a sign of God's favor. Be patient and remain steadfast in your good desires and intentions.

Keep this goal in mind: never let anything undermine your belief in God's love. God is on your side. He wants you to trust Him. He wants you to attain peace of soul. And He wants you to be happy. He and you have basically the same goal.

Q. I believe that, but living it is not as easy as you make it sound.

A. I never said it would be easy. Neither did the Lord. Just know that God is ready to reward every prayer and every gesture of love with new graces. That means your tendency to doubt will be lessened and you will be given greater ability to trust. In time you will see in yourself subtle changes: a more quiet mind and a more loving heart. Surely you can see that you are not the same person you were ten years ago.

Q. Yes, I realize I've changed. Does that mean that the maturing process is also somehow a spiritual thing?

A. It certainly is. Building up your Christian character is a task that requires cooperation with God's grace. We are like the trees. Every tree grows in two directions, and once a tree stops growing, it dies. We can grow in different directions, too.

If you don't have a quiet mind right now, take it one day at a time. Don't ask for tomorrow's graces today. Turn your fears over to the Lord. Let Him carry your burdens for you. Turn your face toward the sun, God's smile, and grow toward Him. Believe that you are God's delight, even though you are far from perfect. Get used to the idea that God's favor is upon you. It will make a tremendous difference in your attitude toward life, pain, temptation, and happiness.

You won't want to displease God. You'll want to delight Him. And what makes all of this so wonderful is that, by desiring to please the Lord, you are already doing just that.

Q. What is prayer? And how do Catholics pray?

A. Prayer is the lifting of the mind and heart to God. The heart often speaks its own language, yearning and pleading in its own way. This is gut-level prayer. However, you must not think that the essence of prayer is in one's emotional response to God. You never have to strain to produce the right set of feelings because true prayer is in the will. Prayer is simply the will to give yourself to God.

Whether a person is alone or in a prayer group, whether the prayer is a part of the liturgy, or a private devotion, it is still "giving yourself to God." Whether one is asking for something, thanking God, pleading for forgiveness or making reparation for sin, it is all a form of self-giving.

There are many prayer traditions in the world. The Eastern traditions of Buddhism and Hinduism are profoundly different from our own. While they are admirable in many ways, we cannot enshrine them as being superior to Christianity. Some types of Eastern meditation *force the meditator to leave behind all that is corporal, even the imagination and concrete concepts. They do this in crass opposition to the doctrine of the Incarnation of God in Christ: everything spiritual in God should become incarnate, and remain so even to the resurrection of the body* (Hans Urs von Balthasar).

Father von Balthasar was one of the great theologians of this century. He died only a few hours before he was to be elevated to the rank of Cardinal by Pope John Paul II. He points out that the central truth of our faith is the Incarnation: God became man in the person of Jesus Christ. The body therefore is an essential part of the human personality, and the body is necessarily involved in the prayer life of every Christian. We use holy objects to remind us of God and the things of God. We touch and look at these holy images in order to be more aware of the mysteries they represent.

The old forms of Platonism and spiritualism which disparage the body's role in favor of some mystical spirituality are foreign to the New Testament. I mention this because Catholics are very much oriented to these holy objects in their devotional life. We make no apology for that, though I can tell you we differ greatly on the things we consider to be aesthetically appealing. There are some holy pictures and statues that really upset me. And I have heard Church music that, were it not for my faith in the Eucharist, would have driven me out of the Church faster than a leaking gas valve.

Catholics do not share the same aesthetic tastes. What works for some is a definite turn-off for others. We do share a common faith, and that faith creates a solidarity which allows freedom within its borders. Unity is not uniformity.

A human being lives his or her spiritual life in a body. Sight and smell are important in our prayer life. We light candles at the altar, offering the sweet aroma of burning wax to the Father as an act of love. This act is a prayer because it is a way of giving yourself to God. Catholics have always prayed in a way that uses the body as an integral part of the worship service. We like to touch things and look at things that remind us of God. Holy water is a sign of purification, incense carries our prayers to heaven along with our hymns of praise. God has no ears. He is pure Spirit. But He reads hearts, and all that we do to communicate with Him is pleasing to Him. It is all part of our self-offering.

(From N.B., Seattle, WA)

There was a time in my life when I reached the end of my rope. My wife had left me. I was a drunk. My kids didn't even want any part of me. I wanted to jump out the window and end it all, when I looked up and saw the crucifix. It brought back a flood of memories of better days when I used to be an altar boy. I kept looking at Christ on the cross, and I broke down and wept. That day my life was changed. In fact, I haven't had a drop for six years. And though I'm not back with my wife, we are at least good friends. I think the Lord spoke to me from the cross that day.

Jesus taught us His greatest lesson from the cross: to accept the situation life hands you, and offer it to God with love. We offer ourselves — mind, heart and will — that God may use us as channels of His mercy and love. We touch the lives of others through prayer and sacrifice.

The Holy Sacrifice of the Mass plays an important role in the devotional life of Catholics because they believe Christ is truly present in the Eucharist. The Eucharist enables us to unite our offering of self to Christ's supreme sacrifice. He only died once, but we recall that death at each Mass knowing that He extends His saving power to us today. The passion and death of Jesus is an eternal act echoing down through history. Jesus said, *Do this in memory of me* (Lk 22:19), and we do.

(From Helen Nikovits, Clifton, NJ)

E   levated bread and wine, consecrated Sacred Food,
U   nbloody sacrifice now made, hidden Calvary is viewed.
C   ommunion with His faithful, as He promised long ago,
H   ere, present on the altar, Christ the Victim's silent show
A   t every Mass, in all the world, reenacted every day,
R   ight before our blessed eyes, greatest miracle comes our way
I   nside our mortal body, we do place Him on a throne.
S   inners, repentant and forgiven, we commune with Him alone.
T   his celebrated conquest, Satan's snare we now resist,
                 Each time we eat at table
                 Sacrificial EUCHARIST!

(From M.A., Miami, FL)

For me, attending daily Mass is a way of saying to God He's "Number One" in my life. I had just returned from Holy Communion one day when I heard this voice within me: "I want you to sacrifice your life for me."

Feeling unworthy, I asked, "Why me?" and the voice answered, "Because all your life you have loved me."

That was true. Even at times when I sinned, I still loved Him.

I was completely baffled. What did it mean? I was married with children. I couldn't become a nun. And a sacrifice is not something I like to make. I went to a priest and told him what happened. He just said, "We have to be careful about such things." For a long time it lingered on my mind. I didn't believe it was my imagination. It was too real. Then one day during Mass the words, "Be a living sacrifice of praise," leaped out at me. Here was my answer, very simply. By attending Holy Mass, as I try to do every day, I believe the Lord is pleased.

(From Mary Tierney, Yonkers, NY)

I believe I delight the Lord when I visit Him in the Blessed Sacrament on Friday evenings. I spend an hour with Him in front of the tabernacle and I praise and thank Him. I come home with peace of mind, joy and hope and love.

The custom of the family rosary is another devotion many Catholics enjoy, although sadly the practice is on the decrease. Those who pray the rosary meditate on the mysteries of Christ's life: the Joyful, Sorrowful and Glorious Mysteries. This devotion creates a special quality of spiritual awareness in the families that practice it.

(From Hanna Ward, Sunnyside, NY)

I was born in a farmhouse in Kerry, Ireland in what I call the happiest family in the world. I thank God for that.

Each night we knelt on the cement floor in front of a fine fire to say the rosary. Eight children and our grandparents lived with us until one of the sons built a house two miles away.

Each night at nine, after the rosary, we brought mother some hot milk or hot chocolate. One night, when I handed her the cup, she fell over unconscious. I tried to reach her, but there was no answer. I thought about what the Poor Clare Sisters taught me, and I whispered an Act of Contrition into her ear.

To this day, I feel that God was pleased with me for helping my mother the way I did.

The practice of saying the family rosary sets up a spiritual awareness that touches every aspect of life. Devotion to the Blessed Virgin Mary is important to Catholics, and rightly so. Mary is the Mother of Jesus. Through the working of the Holy Spirit she brought forth the Son of God from her own body. The Incarnation began in Mary's womb.

Mary is the Spouse of the Holy Spirit and was there at the beginning of the life of the Church. We do not pray to her as though she were an independent deity, but we do value her intercession. We ask her to pray for us because Mary enjoys the privilege of being Christ's mother. This gives her a preeminent place in the life of the Church. We also remember how Jesus deferred to her at the wedding feast of Cana. Mary is not an ordinary woman. The Angel Gabriel addressed these words to her, *Rejoice so highly favored daughter. The Lord is with you* (Lk 1:28).

The Church is made up of real human beings who share in Christ's life. Mary is only one of them but she had a mission from God which did not stop 2000 years ago. She is the Mother of the Church because she is the Mother of God's beloved Son.

You and I have a limited mission to a small circle of people living in our own time. Mary's mission extends to everyone who is touched by her Son. Catholics believe that the radiance of her presence in the world is by God's own design.

Mary has been a source of help and consolation not only to the average person in the average family. She has been a solace to some of the most troubled and abandoned people on earth.

(From Tom Agnelli, Kew Gardens, NY)

I am currently in a psychiatric ward where I am diagnosed as having a schizo-affective disorder. I have been in the hospital for three weeks so far, and I don't mind telling you that without the assistance of Mary (I say a rosary practically every day) I would simply have gone insane a long time ago. The joy I get from prayer is one of the essential oases that helps me make every day productive and helps me to be healed of my problems and shortcomings.

I recognize my need to be here, and only God, working through the empathetic, caring workers here, will help me to find my true potential.

Concerning her mysterious presence in the psyche of Catholics, let me tell you a personal story. I was born on September 8th, the same day we traditionally celebrate the birth of Mary. It wasn't until I became a priest that I learned about my grandmother's devotion to Our Blessed Mother. My mother's mother, Ann Horan, was an Irish immigrant who married Mike Caslin, also right off the boat from Ireland. Together they raised nine children on the Lower East Side of Manhattan. My mother was one of five girls.

I was told by one of my aunts that Grandma prayed all her

life that one of her four sons would be a priest. None were. She also prayed that one of her children would be born on Mary's birthday, September 8th. Here again she was disappointed.

But a generation later, I was born on that day and I can assure you, my grandmother didn't think it was a coincidence. I was about nine months old when she died and, though I have no personal recollection of her, I have seen snapshots of her holding me as an infant. I can imagine what she was praying for as she rocked me to sleep.

There's no doubt in my mind that her prayers were a powerful influence in my life. I was ordained a priest on May 28th, 1960, after a long struggle to discern my place in the world. I didn't have a clue that someone else might have been praying for me during that struggle. I was totally under the impression that the whole idea of my vocation was between me and God alone. My mother never mentioned any of this to me. She died in 1957.

Catholics do not make the Blessed Virgin into the Mediator between God and man. Jesus Christ alone is our Mediator and Savior. But we do give Mary special respect. Because she brought us the Mediator, she is called the Mediatrix. Her words, recorded in Scripture, are few and far between. Remember what she said to the waiters at the marriage feast of Cana, just before Jesus turned the water into wine: *Go and do whatever He tells you* (Jn 2:5). That sentence sums up her message to us today.

Mary brings Jesus to us. And she brings us to Jesus.

Catholics also believe in the Communion of Saints, and that means they believe that those who have gone before us are still taking care of us in their own way. What a delightful thought.

I think it pleases the Lord when our faith reaches out beyond the narrow confines of our personal lives to include the vast outreaches of possibility. Imagine a great, great, great,

great grandmother in heaven who is praying for you right now. Even though you don't know her personally, she knows you, and she is praying for your salvation every day. It's mind-boggling, isn't it?

We think of Mary as a spiritual relative. Indeed, we believe that our Lord gave her to us as our spiritual mother when, from the cross, He said to John, *Behold your mother* and to Mary, *Behold your son* (Jn 19:26-27). Jesus is our Brother and, by Baptism, we are the adopted children of God the Father. This makes us brothers and sisters of one another.

The following is an aid to prayer. I don't know who wrote it, but I've used it for years myself and others have found it most helpful. Imagine the Lord speaking directly to you:

You don't have to be clever to please Me. Just speak to Me as you would to anyone who cares about you.

Are there any people you want to pray for? Tell Me their names and ask for as much as you want. I am generous. Trust Me to do what I know is best.

Tell Me about your pride, your touchiness, your self-centeredness, your laziness. I still love you in spite of all your faults. Do not be ashamed in My presence. There were many saints in heaven who had the same faults as you. They prayed, and little by little their faults were corrected.

Do not hesitate to ask for blessings for body and mind, for health, memory and success. I can give everything.

Tell Me about your failures, and I will show you the cause of them. What are your worries? Who has caused you pain? Tell Me about it. Forgive them and I will bless you.

Are you afraid of anything? Have you any tormenting, unreasonable fears? Trust yourself to Me. I am here and will not leave you.

Have you no joys to share with Me? Tell Me about them. What has happened since yesterday to cheer your spirit and comfort you? Whatever it was, big or small, remember that I prepared it for you. Show Me your gratitude.

Are there temptations bearing heavily upon you? Yielding to them always disturbs the peace of your soul. Ask Me, and I will help you overcome them.

Well, go along now. Get on with your work or play. Try to be humbler, more submissive, kinder to others. Come back soon and bring Me a more devoted heart. Tomorrow I shall have more blessings for you.

(From Mary Kathleen Foster, Salisbury, MD)

In the pre-dawn dark, Dad would wake me with a gentle tug and a soft word. We were making nine Tuesdays: Mass, communion, and prayers in honor of St. Anthony, asking to help Dad find a job. Dressing quickly to change from the warmth of the bed to my cold clothes, I cherished each Tuesday as a special time of closeness to God. We were living in the Depression of the 30's and Dad was almost sixty. I was about twelve.

We walked the six city blocks to Holy Redeemer in the frigid Ohio winter, chattering like birds about our supernal speculations regarding Jesus and His friends. Some Tuesdays we traveled as mute as two monks dawdling along to morning prayers, sharing their heavy silence. Sometimes deep snows and biting winds made us wool-up with extra sweaters and mufflers and shoe-up with layers of socks. Shoving his bare hands deep into his overcoat pockets, Dad aimed his body board-like into the wind. Considerately, a few early cars had left narrow tire tracks in the streets. He chose one as his path and was off like a wind gust, shouting words of encouragement and shielding his small coat-tail buddy behind him.

On easier days, he acquainted me with the prayers and practices in the small brown pamphlet that guided our novena. He explained all, carefully gearing his words to my child's mind. A special gift found its way to us through our rapport: the adventure of finding our Creator in the lives of the saints who had shared our humanity. If one could love God so much more by an acquaintance with this gentle Saint Anthony, we reasoned, what raptures lie ahead in learning the friendships that existed between Him and all the others whose names had Saint before them. What a great challenge it was! What a sweet pursuit it still is! What a magnificent heavenly block-party it will be!

CHAPTER ELEVEN

Strive To Please The Lord

Take care to live in Me, and let Me live in you we read in the Gospel of St. John (15:4). St. Therese of Lisieux, the Little Flower, lived in Jesus and devoted herself to the fulfillment of his commandment of love by performing little acts of charity and placing them like flowers at the feet of the Master. She learned the joy of giving joy to her neighbor and thereby pleasing the Father. As she wrote, *Great saints worked for the glory of God, but I, who am only a little soul, work only to please Him. . . . I have always remained little, with no other occupation than gathering flowers, flowers of love and sacrifice, and offering them to God in order to please Him.*

In a letter to her sister Leonie, she continued the theme: *If you want to be a saint, it will be quite easy. Set yourself only one aim: to please Jesus.*

Father Paul De Jaegher, S.J., commenting on the charism of St. Therese wrote, "All this does not mean, however, that the soul always experiences, in an emotionally perceptible way, the delightful heavenly joy of pleasing her divine spouse. Such a thing is impossible. The heart of a creature could never in this life contain so much happiness."

He goes on to explain that the joy St. Therese experienced was hidden in the depth of her soul, and that at times admitted of aridity. He wanted to point out the danger of becoming too attached to our good feelings. Nevertheless, we have the good example of St. Therese to spur us on. With or without good feelings we can offer our little flowers to the Lord, day by day.

Another great woman who thought in the same way, not a Catholic but a saint in her own right, was Helen Keller. Blind from birth she grew in wisdom, age and grace. Here is my favorite quote from her journal:

> *I long to accomplish a great and noble task,*
> *but it is my chief duty to accomplish*
> *humble tasks as though they were great and noble.*
> *The world is moved along,*
> *not only by the mighty shoves of its heroes*
> *but also by the aggregate*
> *of the tiny pushes of each honest worker.*

Helen Keller lived in a world of darkness. She could have ended up a wretched crank, but the Lord graced her with a grateful heart.

There are times in the life of good people that can only be described as miserable. Life gets complicated very easily. Some of the little flowers we offer to God may grow thorns. People resent the things we do for all kinds of reasons. In the confusion, feelings of joy tend to dissolve. It would be risky to depend on them.

Try to remember that your little love offerings are more precious in times of stress. The Lord reads hearts. He knows your good intentions.

Pleasing the Lord is following your conscience.

(From V.M., no address)

It's difficult to write this without feeling we are boasting, but there was a time when a young girl I knew and loved as though she were my daughter was going through a difficult time. She dated a relative of mine and betrayed him. Of course, as a result, he wanted nothing to do with her. She became despondent and had a nervous breakdown.

I became terribly upset because of her condition, and I continued to show love and care for her, offering many prayers on her behalf. My relative became annoyed with me because I continued my friendship with her. He felt I was being disloyal to him, but I could not help but be concerned for her and continue my love and prayers. To make a long story short, she finally recovered from her depression.

Even though I loved this relative of mine very much, I felt I had done the right thing in being concerned about the girl and showing it.

Pleasing the Lord in little ways is the goal of Christian spirituality. We are asked to make the sacrifices necessary to become as little children. This idea means different things to different people, but the underlying common thread is our humble belief that God is present and intimately involved in everything we experience.

Pleasing the Lord is accepting your cross.

(From Geraldine Raineri, Paterson, NJ)

On November 4, 1988 I was admitted to the hospital with a condition of the ear called "chrondritis." My right ear had swelled overnight to twice its normal size, was reddish-purple and felt as though it would surely explode at any moment. The ear specialist advised me that my ear would never look normal again, and that I had a severe staph infection which had devastated the soft tissue and the cartilage of the ear. I was told that I would probably need surgery and that I was being placed on high doses of antibiotics intravenously.

Self-pity began to creep in but, before it infected my mind, I decided to pray with complete faith and confidence that medical probabilities and divine possibilities are not always the same. I talked with God with the faith and trust of a little child going to her father and believing in his love and goodness, that no matter what, only good would come out of all this. I believed with all my heart that God would heal me or give me the grace to accept my ear, however it looked. I think that God was delighted with my simple childlike prayer. I think He was happy to see me go to Him just as I once approached Santa. . . .

My spirit remained uplifted despite many painful treatments and unpleasant hospital experiences. I felt an inner peace, joy and freedom that defy description. I delighted in trusting God with all my heart and truly placing myself in His care.

It is almost a year since my ten-day hospitalization. My experience taught me that God's grace doesn't come necessarily through happy events, wrapped in pretty paper and tied with beautiful bows, but rather His grace frequently comes through the crosses, the trials and roadblocks that are part of everyone's life.

I never did need surgery and the doctors called my recovery "dramatic" and "remarkable." My right ear matches my left one. I beat the medical probabilities and am a living testimony to the divine possibilities. I believe that God is delighted every time I put on earrings and cut my hair short with my ears plainly visible and obviously normal after all. What father wouldn't be delighted to see his child happy and well and ever grateful to be alive to rejoice in another day which the Lord has made?

Pleasing the Lord is caring for God's little creatures.

(From J.S.W., Springfield, IL)

There are lots of times when I sense the Lord delights in me. For example, I have lots of little pets that depend on me to care for them, and I think the Lord delights in my tender care. I think the Lord smiles at me when He sees how normal it is for me to do this.

Pleasing the Lord is being playful with God.

(Anonymous)

I was alone after a prayerful hour while on retreat. I was drawn to a tall grove of trees away from the bench where I was sitting. At the start of the path, I found a new, yellow tennis ball which I immediately picked up. Despite the fact that I was a grown, middle-aged woman with nine children, I decided to play with my beloved God. I tossed the ball up in the air and God tossed it back to me. Up and down . . . gravity was not considered. It was the Lord and I at play. When we finished, I was filled with gratitude for the joy and delight I had been given. However, it took three more years to realize that I had delighted Him.

Pleasing the Lord is learning how to forgive.

(From Georgine Ashworth, Lawrence, KS)

After my divorce, I was angry, bitter, and filled with resentment and hatred for my ex-husband. I went through all the "How could you let this happen to me, Lord?" and "Where are you, Lord, now that I need you?" feelings.

Somewhere along the healing road that I was traveling, it became apparent that I needed to express myself to my Father in heaven, as a child of His truly would. I cried, sobbed, moaned and groaned. I beat my breast and asked for forgiveness for the feelings I had toward my ex-husband, and for the anger. I prayed aloud one sleepless night, "Father, forgive me. I want to trust and believe and have faith like a child, but right now I don't. Please help me to realize that there is life after divorce. And help me really mean what I am about to say: I want to truly wish my ex-husband and his new wife all the best that life has to offer. You know I don't mean this now. But I want to."

My Father in heaven is loving enough to forgive me. He listens to me and I have developed a very personal relationship with my Lord as a result. I am unconditionally acceptable to Him and I love it. I still slip every now and then, but I know He picks me up and He is there saying, "It's OK. I am with you."

**Pleasing the Lord is performing the duties
of your state in life cheerfully.**

(From P.W.K., Boston, MA)

Although I don't like to study and even though I finish my required homework every night at my mother's request, I spend a minimum of two hours a night studying or reading to please my mother. And that also benefits me because doing at least two hours of homework a night becomes a good habit which helps me in my school work. So by doing it, I not only please my Mom and my teachers, but hopefully, God as well.

Pleasing the Lord is working through grief.

(From Joan Savio, Brooklyn, NY)

When my husband Donald died five and one-half years ago, I felt like I wanted to die too. We were so close, so in love. How could I go on without him? I talked it over with God and told Him how I felt as I cried many tears. But God let me know that He wanted me to live because my work on earth was not yet finished. He reminded me that as much as I loved Donald, my life was separate from his.

God was right because, although I still love and miss my husband, my best friend, I'm no longer unhappy because I'm busy reaching out, trying to do God's will for me. In the process of healing and growing, I have become a joyful and fulfilled person. Instead of giving up, I gave in to become the person God wanted me to be. I'm sure God is delighted with me, because now others will see His light shining in me and through me.

Pleasing the Lord is enjoying your work.

(From Vicky Cutchlow, Kent, WA)

I think my attitude about work delights the Lord. I'm a real estate agent and I pray the Lord to bless my efforts on behalf of my customers and only bring me those whom I will bless or who will bless me . . . I feel such freedom and such joy. Words are inadequate.

Pleasing the Lord is allowing Him to make you an instrument of His love.

(From Kathy Bombace, Ocala, FL)

God our Father delights in me when I recognize that I'm the instrument through which His love flows to others, and when I allow this to happen I, too, feel His abundant love.

God takes delight in me when I pray, believing and expecting the very best.

Pleasing the Lord is doing little things to please one's neighbor.

(From José de Vinck, Allendale, NJ)

As I was about to enter a delicatessen, a tall black man unloading a trailer-truck asked me for a cigarette. I told him I was sorry, I didn't smoke. I bought a pack of cigarettes in the deli, and while the man was rummaging inside the truck, I placed it on the tailgate. As my car pulled out alongside the truck, I saw him gape at the apparition. He spotted me smiling as I drove away, and he got the point. His wave and grin were the best return I ever received for such a small investment.

There are many voices but one Spirit behind all these testimonies. It is the Holy Spirit who teaches us that it's not how much you do, it's how much love you put into the doing. Jesus tells us that at the Last Judgment, we will be rewarded: *Because you have been faithful over a little, I will set you over much; enter into the joy of your master* (Mt 25:21).

A crowd gathered around Jesus and a woman who had heard of His reputation as a healer touched the fringe of His garment, hoping to be cured of the bleeding that troubled her for twelve years. The touch could have gone unnoticed in the crowd, but Jesus sensed it and, turning to the woman, said, *Your faith has made you well* (Mt 9:22).

At another time, Jesus was teaching in the temple and He saw the way people were putting money into the temple treasury. Many rich people put in large sums, but then a poor widow came along and put in two copper coins. He noticed this and said to His disciples: *This poor widow has put in more than all those who are contributing to the treasury. For they are giving out of their abundance; but she, out of her poverty, has put in everything she had* (Lk 21:4).

Little things do make a difference. A personal God sees all, and rewards us according to the purity of our hearts.

It was Rosa Parks' resolve not to sit in the back of the bus that gave rise to the civil rights movement and thrust Martin Luther King Jr. to the forefront of American history.

Ralph Waldo Emerson said, "The creation of a thousand forests is in one acorn." President Calvin Coolidge put the same idea another way: "People criticize me for harping on the obvious. Perhaps some day I'll write an article on the importance of the obvious. If all the folks in the United States would do the few simple things they know they ought to do, most of our big problems would take care of themselves."

Here are some little things that matter.

Kind words. "What is the secret of your marriage?" a reporter asked a couple on their 50th wedding anniversary. The husband answered, "After the wedding, my father-in-law gave me a gold pocket watch. Inscribed on it were the words, 'Say something nice to Sarah.' I saw that reminder every day and followed its advice."

A warm greeting. Richard Levangie, writing in the *Catholic Digest*, tells of his depression over the deaths of his father and a close friend. One day, feeling empty, he went to Mass in a strange church and sat off to the side. "Two elderly women hobbled over to my solitary corner. Their journey seemed to take forever, and yet their greeting was warm and

caring. In the moment it took them to arrive, I made the
decision to rejoin the living."

A promise kept.   In 1955 the son of the founder of a
Georgia real estate firm deposited $300,000 in a bank to repay
some 500 stockholders who had lost money when the firm
failed. The deposit fulfilled a promise made by his father 28
years earlier. Johnny Mercer had become a song writer and he
never forgot his dad's promise. Mercer wrote many songs;
among them was "Accentuate the Positive." Making dreams
come true takes a little perseverance.

A can of food.   When Robert Simon and Celine Burk
married, they requested that the guests bring some canned
goods to the reception. "Help us to share our joy with others,"
they asked. The food was to be distributed to the poor, "as an
extension of our love."

Respect for self.   Anthony Muñoz, the all-pro lineman for
the Cincinnati Bengals, once declined a request for an in-
terview by *Playboy* magazine. Muñoz said the magazine's
values were not his values: "With my beliefs as a Christian, I
couldn't see doing it."

Small talk.   At a father-and-son banquet at which he
was to speak, Yogi Berra was happily signing baseball bats for
his young fans. He noticed a group of lads off to the side who
had no gifts. He was told they were from a nearby orphanage.
Berra left his table and went over to them to sign their prog-
rams. When one of the organizers asked him to return to the
head table and say a few words, Berra told him, "Go on with the
program. I'm busy talking to some friends."

The Lord notices the little things because they mean a lot
to some people. And what you do for them you do for Him.

There are many others who have expressed similar ideas.
Here are just a few:

Democracy is not measured by its leaders doing extraordi-

*nary things, but by its citizens doing ordinary things extraordi-
narily well.* John W. Gardner

Nothing that can please the heart of the Lord is small. St.
Madeleine Barat

*In the joy of little things the heart finds its morning and is
refreshed.* Kahlil Gibran

*Each of us can do a little to bring some portion of misery to
an end.* Albert Schweitzer

*The kingdom of heaven is like a grain of mustard seed
which a man took and sowed in his field. It is the smallest of all
seeds, but when it has grown it is the greatest of shrubs and
becomes a tree.* Mt 13:31

> Dear Father in heaven,
> author of all holiness,
> please enlighten my mind
> so that I may dream up little ways
> of delighting You.
> Protect me and help me
> to persevere in my good intentions
> and instill in me an awareness of Your smile.

(The following testimonies are by teenagers from St. Brigid's parish, Boston, MA, courtesy of Sister M. Loretto Tucker)

1. Sometimes you are able to please God without even realizing that you're doing it. One time I remember a friend of mine was responsible for baking something for a fair. Just the night before, she realized that she did not have the time or supplies that she needed. That night, I baked the cookies for her and brought them over to her in the morning. She was very relieved and her gratitude and appreciation for what I had done was well worth the effort.

A.M.S.

2. There was one event that pleased God more than the other small things I have done. I signed up for a fund-raising "Walk-for-Hunger." I thought it would be easy, but while I was walking the twenty miles and seeing thousands of people walking with me, I realized how important each one of the people walking really was, including me, because we were walking for each hungry person in America. These thoughts gave me really good feelings to finish the long walk and to aid the many people who are hungry. Now I look forward to community service to others rather than putting it off.

C.J.W.

3. A time when I think I pleased God was when I was late for class and saw an underclassman drop his book bag. Despite the fact I was late, I helped him to pick up his belongings. In doing so, I felt good about myself for the rest of the day.

E.R.B.

CHAPTER TWELVE

Go Forth and Teach

There is a reciprocal relationship between God and creation. We only have to look at the world about us to see how the Father depends on us to fulfill His plan. Just as the soil needs tilling to produce a good harvest, so too human beings need to be taught in order to come to a knowledge of the truth. That's why Jesus invites us all to *go into the whole world and preach the good news to every creature* (Mk 16:15), to *go and seek what has gone astray* (Mt 18:12), and to *go along the valleys and the by-ways urging the people to come in, so that My house may be full* (Lk 14:23).

There are many ways we can perform this service. Every time we speak of God reverently to another person we awaken mysterious forces within them. We become carriers of divine truth.

(From Mary Nina Melendez, New York, NY)

One night a few weeks ago it was raining very hard, so I decided to take a cab home. I noticed that the driver had a statue of the Blessed Virgin and a crucifix on the dashboard. I saw my chance to stimulate the driver's faith in God, but I wasn't sure how to do it. I knew the Lord would provide the opportunity.

Suddenly a young man crossing the street against the light stepped in front of the cab. The driver almost went through the windshield.

"Some people are stupid enough to jump in front of cars in order to collect insurance money," he said. "Life for them has no value."

I told him that I had been in a very bad accident and no money in the world could compensate for physical injuries. My snowmobile accident had almost cost me my life, but the Lord saw fit to spare me. I then told him all the details of my accident. The driver was mesmerized by my story as he listened quietly. Then I came to the moment that I refer to as "crossing over to the other side." Upon the impact of my snowmobile with the barbed wire fence, I fell into a pleasant darkness — no pain, no sorrow, no pleasure. I just floated in the darkness of the universe. Then, coming from my left side, a beam of light crossed my vision. It looked like a green comet and on the tip was an embryo, a baby, a little girl, a teenager, a young woman, until finally I recognized myself. My entire life passed before me in a fraction of a second. I remember thinking that I must be dead. "Jesus," I yelled. "Jesus, come and get me." Then it was as if I had been in a dark closet and the door had been kicked open. An immense light shone on me. It was so powerful I could not look at it. I perceived a message in my mind . . . as though God were saying: "You have a son to raise, things to do, paintings to create, and testimonies to give. Your time is not up."

I had the sensation of falling back to earth and I woke up in the rescue ambulance. My hands and feet were tied together because I was given up for dead. "No money in the world could compensate for life," I told the driver. Just then we pulled up to my house. "How much do I owe you for the ride?" "Nothing, Señora," he said. He gave me his card and offered his service any time, day or night. Then he picked up the crucifix from the dashboard and kissed it.

I knew then and there that the Lord was delighted with me.

The Father wants us to help one another in our spiritual growth. That doesn't necessarily mean preaching on a soap box, but it does mean sharing our faith experience with those who are disposed to listen. The Kingdom of Heaven is His gift to those who believe. We please the Lord when we share our faith with others.

Human beings need shelter, clothing, and food in order to have basic human dignity. All of us need a just society in order to live in peace and harmony with our neighbor. We need a loving family environment if we are to experience joy and become carriers of divine love.

Jesus asks us to care about one another as we build up the Kingdom. This is our mission. It is also the sign of our love: *By this you will know My disciples, that they love one another* (Jn 13:35). Jesus not only expects us to love one another, He promises that our reward in heaven will be based on the quality of our love: *When I was hungry you gave Me food; when I was thirsty you gave Me a drink* (Mt 25:35). We have this amazing capacity to please the Lord when we tend to the needs of others because He is there, within them.

(From Allison Gallimelli, teenager, Boston, MA)

I know God is pleased when my friend and I volunteer at the hospital. We do many things for the sick and helpless. I enjoy volunteering because I know it helps people who can't get out of bed, to help the nurses who have so many things to do, and just be kind and friendly to people. I think God and the people at the hospital are proud to have someone come in and help out.

Good example is the most effective form of preaching the Gospel.

By helping others, even without consciously doing it with Christ in mind, we satisfy God's command and we delight Him. Charity overcomes a multitude of sins. By emptying ourselves, giving up time and energy to be there for others, we are imitating Jesus who did everything to please the Father. The Father is delighted with those who sacrifice themselves in this way.

The *corporal* works of mercy are concerned with feeding the hungry, giving drink to the thirsty, clothing the naked, etc. There are also the *spiritual* works of mercy: admonishing sinners (not an easy thing to do), instructing the ignorant, counselling the doubtful, comforting the sorrowful, bearing wrongs patiently, forgiving injuries, praying for the living and the dead.

Comforting the sorrowful can take many forms. One of them is soothing the pain of the grief-stricken.

(From Jolene Brown, Topeka, KS)

One of the young men in our parish had just started his freshman year in college and was home for Labor Day weekend. He was killed in a car wreck returning home from the lake one evening. I was a youth minister at the parish and with some of his classmates planned the music for the liturgy. It was difficult for all of us, but I feel we were very supportive for the family. The day before the funeral I wrote a poem and dedicated it to Jim. I wanted to share it with the family but kept putting it off. Finally four or five months later, I made myself take it to his mom.

The day I took it was Jim's birthday! I had no idea . . . what a strange feeling. I guess God does work little miracles in our lives if we just listen and let Him. Situations like this are very difficult and we often avoid the family because we are hurting or we don't know what to say.

You don't have to say anything, really, just be. This is what the experts say. I think God delights in each of us when we reach out and allow the Holy Spirit to work through us.

The Spirit leads us in different ways to minister to one another. Ministering is a form of evangelization. That word is a turn-off for many. In the strict sense it means, "to preach the Gospel, or to convert people to Christ." There are some sects that force their way on others and, though they are zealous, their efforts are often counter-productive. Fools rush in where angels fear to tread. Evangelization need not be threatening. We preach the Gospel most effectively by the way we live. There are times, however, when we can and should speak up for Christ.

Standing up for our beliefs is needed more than ever in this day and age when religion is so often treated with scorn. We have to do more than simply let it pass. It's a cop-out to remain passive, saying that religion is a private matter, so it's none of my business what anyone else says about it.

It does matter! If someone dares to insult Almighty God, or Jesus, or the Church, that insult should not go unchallenged. God's friendship is personal, and friends stand up for one another. Jesus said, *You are the salt of the earth. If you lose your flavor, what will happen to the world? . . . You are the light of the world. A city on top of a hill cannot be hidden, nor do men light a lamp to place it under a basket: they set it on a stand where it shines for everyone in the house. In the same way let your good deeds shine for all to see, so as to give glory to your Father in Heaven* (Mt 5:13-16).

It is a spiritual work of mercy to speak up for your faith. It's part of the virtue of religion.

A believer and a skeptic went for a walk together. The skeptic said, "Look at the trouble and misery of the world. After thousands of years of religion it's no better. What good is religion?" The believer thought for a moment and then pointed to a child, filthy with grime, playing in the gutter. He said, "We've had soap for generations too, and yet look how dirty that child is." The skeptic protested, "But soap can't do any good unless it's used." "Exactly so," replied the believer. "And the same is true of religion."

Religion is something that everyone needs, but many do not know how much they need it. How do you convince them without being obnoxious and turning them further away from God? There is an art to it.

As Jesus completed His time on earth He had a few things to say about this: *Go and make disciples in every nation, baptizing them in the name of the Father and of the Son and of the Holy Spirit. Teach them to obey all the commands I have given you, and remember I will be with you always until the end of the world* (Mt 28:19-20). And again, *As the branch cannot bear fruit on its own but must remain on the vine, neither can you unless you abide in Me. I am the vine; you are the branches. He who abides in Me and I in him will bear much fruit. Without Me, though, you are nothing* (Jn 15:4-5).

We are called to be evangelizers in this world: *You did not choose Me. I chose you and established you that you may go and bring forth fruit, fruit that will last* (Jn 15:16). To do this, there are times when we have to take the initiative and invite people to pray with us, or come to church with us, or minister to others with us.

(From Roger Matyss, Belgium, Europe)

We have the custom in our family of praying the FIAT Rosary every night. The idea is to unite ourselves with our Blessed Mother. We pray with her to the Holy Spirit, the way she prayed with the Apostles before Pentecost. We pray for the courage to be apostles in the world. We believe that God wants us to make Jesus more widely known and loved.

I encourage my children to do little things on their own to accomplish this goal. One of my sons decided he wanted to go to Mass one day each week in addition to Sunday. He began getting up early every Friday morning, and on his own went off to Mass. After a few months, his best friend became aware of his devotion, and asked about it. My son encouraged him to come along and try it. With that the two of them began going together. This in turn attracted others who were invited into the little club, and today several boys are going to Mass every Friday morning. What I like is that two of them came from families where no one even went to Mass on Sunday. Now the boys are influencing their brothers and sisters to go, at least on Sundays.

You don't have to get on a soap-box to influence others. Prayer and a caring attitude can make a tremendous difference.

Let me tell you about FIAT. In 1980 Cardinal Suenens, the retired Catholic Primate of Belgium, asked me to travel with him from Rome to the United States. He was invited to the annual meeting of the House of Bishops of the Episcopal Church to conduct a holy hour for them each morning before their deliberations began. This ecumenical gesture was inspired by the close friendship the Cardinal had with the late Archbishop Ramsey of Canterbury, England, who was the head of the Anglican Church at the same time Cardinal Suenens was one of the main moderators at the Second Vatican Council.

I joined the Cardinal in Rome and was doubly thrilled when the Cardinal brought me to meet Pope John Paul II. It was a memorable visit. I concelebrated Mass the next morning with the Cardinal and the Pope in his private chapel. I'll never forget it.

Later that day, flying over the Atlantic, Cardinal Suenens explained his dream to me. He believed that the Second Vatican Council only began the process of awakening the laity, whom he called "a sleeping giant." He was convinced that the Church could no longer depend on a few thousand missionary priests and religious to convert the world to Christ. The spirit of secularism was so wide-spread that a mighty effort was needed by everyone, carrying their own weight, to change the spiritual climate of the world.

To be a Christian is to be a missionary. Millions of souls are falling away from religion in this secular world of ours, and too few of God's children are doing anything about it.

During the last ten years of his life, the Cardinal developed a program, "a pastoral initiative" as he called it, to strengthen the fervor and resolve of lay people in making Christ better known and loved in the world. It is a network of informal prayer groups called FIAT.

Cardinal Suenens contacted me originally because he was a friend of the late Father James Keller, my predecessor and the founder of The Christophers. During the Second Vatican Council they collaborated often, and the Cardinal learned about The Christophers. Every week of the year, through our television, radio and print ministries, we reach out to millions of people in 125 nations with the message of the Gospel. We believe that each person has a God-given mission in this world, a job to do that nobody else can do. The Lord asks each one of us to make His concern for the salvation of the world our own.

Pope John Paul II issued an apostolic exhortation on the laity in 1989 entitled *Christifideles Laici*. It reaffirmed the laity's secular mission to become actively engaged in their responsibilities in the professional, social, cultural and political world. In simple words, to take Christ with you wherever you go.

When the Cardinal asked me to help him spread his

"FIAT prayer group" concept throughout North America, I was honored, and a little overwhelmed. I happily accepted the challenge. In the next few years I met with FIAT leaders from France, Belgium, Holland, Spain and England. I asked Msgr. John Demkovich to be my Associate Director, and the two of us attended meetings with Cardinal Suenens and his associates in France during August, 1988. With the permission of my bishop, The Most Rev. Frank J. Rodimer of Paterson, NJ, we established the U.S. headquarters of FIAT at 63 Monroe St., Passaic, NJ 07055.

Each FIAT prayer group is Christ-centered, with our Blessed Mother as our model of obedience. The word FIAT is taken from Mary's own words, spoken under the inspiration of the Holy Spirit to the Angel Gabriel at the Annunciation: *Be it done unto me according to your word* (Lk 1:38). In Latin, the phrase reads: *Fiat mihi secundum verbum tuum.* Mary's "Fiat," or "Yes" to God, is our inspiration.

Members of each FIAT prayer group pledge to meet at least once a month. Some meet biweekly and others weekly. It's entirely up to the local chapter. The size of each group varies from three to twelve. There are no hard-and-fast rules, no dues or obligations. Each person is free to participate according to his or her own level of comfort. The Cardinal insisted that we keep the rules flexible so the focus would be on the connection between prayer and apostolic action rather than on rules and regulations.

He also asked that we pray the FIAT rosary, and try to bring together the idea of Mary and the Holy Spirit. He felt many Protestants think that Catholics make too much of Mary, and many Catholics think that Protestants minimize her role in God's plan of redemption. Pope John Paul II urged us to enter the cenacle with Mary and pray for an outpouring of the Holy Spirit upon the Church and the world. We are trying to do that.

There is an opening prayer to the FIAT rosary which

Cardinal Suenens wrote to capture the idea of praying with
Mary:

> *Most Holy Spirit, help us to relive, in union with Mary,*
> *the Joyful, Sorrowful and Glorious Mysteries of Jesus Christ.*
> *Grant that we may be*
> *— inspired by the faith of our Baptism,*
> *— nourished by the Eucharist,*
> *— and renewed in the grace of Pentecost*
> *so as to live, in word and deed,*
> *always and everywhere,*
> *as faithful witnesses of Christ and of the*
> *love of His divine heart. Amen.*

We are called to witness to God's love, but witnessing is
never easy.

After the death of Jesus, the Apostles were terrified. They
had been warned that if they kept up their preaching about
Jesus, they too might be crucified. Frightened and confused,
the group met in the Upper Room. With Mary in their midst,
they all prayed for divine help.

As she prayed with the Apostles, the Holy Spirit de-
scended upon them. Twelve frightened men emerged from that
experience strengthened and emboldened to preach the
Gospel to all nations. The Church was born that Pentecost, and
the Holy Spirit continues to come to our assistance today,
bringing the fire of divine love into our hearts.

Cardinal Suenens is asking us to pray to the Holy Spirit in
the same way, in union with Mary, and to accomplish this he
designed the FIAT Rosary, which is prayed at every FIAT
meeting. Pope John Paul II gave him permission to promote
this rosary which is shorter than the traditional rosary. By
reducing the number of "Hail Mary's" which are said at each
mystery, the focus is more on the mystery of Christ's life itself.

The Joyful Mysteries are the Annunciation, the Visitation, and the Nativity. The Sorrowful Mysteries are the Agony of Jesus, the Carrying of the Cross, and the Crucifixion. The Glorious Mysteries are the Resurrection, the Descent of the Holy Spirit Upon the Apostles, and the Assumption. At every mystery we say three Hail Mary's and a Glory Be. The final prayer is as follows:

O Mary, teach us how to say "YES" to the Lord,
O Mary, every moment of our life.

O Mary, teach us how to say "THANK YOU" to the Lord,
O Mary, every moment of our life.

At each FIAT meeting, after praying the rosary, a group discussion follows. Each member of the prayer group is invited to tell about a moment in the past week when he or she tried to make Christ better known and loved. No one has to report if they prefer not to, but generally, in time, even the most timid soul in the group joins in. Graces flow abundantly at these meetings.

Concerning evangelization itself, we all must proceed at our own pace. Sometimes others are touched that you care about them. Some are quite open to an invitation to speak about their deeper feelings. Some are even ripe for an invitation to a day of recollection, or a special church service. It never hurts to ask.

Very often when I'm with someone I've met for the first time, I get around to asking the question, "Are you a person of faith?" It's fascinating what this question does to open up a spiritual conversation. I asked an actress the question once, and she answered, "No, I'm not. But I wish I were." We talked about it for some time, and I was amazed at how receptive she was about getting her life back together in the Lord. Asking questions can lead to many other graces. All you need is a little nerve, and the good sense to back off if the person is not receptive. A general rule of thumb is this: never be intrusive, but "let your light shine."

On the other hand, there is such a thing as crisis intervention. You may see such a glaring need at some point that you'll know you should say something. At that point, a little boldness is quite in order. In fact it can be a real gift of love. It's never inappropriate to show that you care. Many times the person will politely put you off, but you started them thinking and it's surprising what can happen as a result of a polite question.

What's so difficult about wanting to share the joy of your faith with another human being? If they'd rather not talk about it, fine. At least you gave them a chance; at least you had the right intention. Pope Pius XII once wrote, "The Catholic spirit is the missionary spirit."

There are many FIAT prayer groups around the world today, and we find they are flourishing on their own without much help from any central office. Each one takes on a personality of its own. This is as it should be, since each group is autonomous. The encouragement the members give to one another is inspiring.

God doesn't force His grace upon us, but we grow in grace when we open our hearts to His initiatives. Helping others in this way is a spiritual work of mercy.

The purpose of the FIAT prayer group, therefore, is to help the members of the group to pray together for the grace to overcome inertia. Inertia leads to a kind of torpor that keeps people timid and isolated from others. "There is a great inertia in the Church that does not like to be disturbed," wrote Hans Urs von Balthasar. Grace overcomes inertia. Pray for the grace to do a little more than you are presently doing.

If you would like to start a FIAT prayer group in your home, or be part of a group, write to me, care of FIAT at the above address and I'll send you some information on it. Call a friend and talk it over. Or if the time isn't right, be patient. God will let you know when to make your move. When you do, you can be sure the Lord will be delighted.

A letter came to me recently which described one man's view of how God's grace works in our lives. I found it quite fascinating.

A few years ago I was faced with a difficult career decision. Two paths lay before me. My prayer was distracted by the notion that whichever path I chose, perhaps God wanted something else.

As I struggled with this, I suddenly envisioned a new image of God, a rather unconventional image: that of a shoe salesman. A good shoe salesman lays out the different types of shoes, encouraging the buyer to try on each pair, to get a feel for each. The good salesman doesn't force a pair of shoes on the buyer; he only wants what is really best for the person who has to wear the shoes. The good salesman's consuming interest is to have the buyer walk away happy. The good salesman delights in the customer's delight once the decision is made.

God is that way, too. And once I realized that, I was able to relax and truly discern the way for me to go.

In the matter of evangelization you should only do what feels comfortable for you. Take one grace at a time. Actual grace is a light to the mind or an impulse to the will. We have to discern what is really from God, and what is not, before attempting any new endeavor.

Those who do too much on their own run the risk of suffering burnout. But when the initiative is inspired by God, all the obstacles and difficulties only spur us on to greater zeal. Pleasing the Lord is not as difficult as you may think.

Here are the *Seven Pillars of FIAT Spirituality*:

1. Pray for the grace to overcome all sin.

2. As you awaken each morning, make a solemn sign of the cross and recite one Our Father. Offer the Lord all the joys and sufferings of the coming day.

3. Attend daily Mass, and if this is not possible, review the scripture readings of the Mass of the day.

4. Create a prayer corner in your home with your favorite picture of Jesus on display. Spend some quiet time there each day in prayer and spiritual reading.

5. Recite the FIAT rosary daily, uniting with Mary before the Holy Spirit, recalling the story of Christ's mission on earth: to save us and to proclaim God's love to the world.

6. Join a few other friends of like mind and meet together at least once a month to encourage one another to be modern day apostles. Rely on the Holy Spirit. He will guide you.

7. Witness to the Good News of God's love and mercy by living gladly because of the knowledge of His love.

For those members of FIAT prayer groups who would like to make a deeper commitment, here is a formula written by Cardinal Suenens.

Most Holy Spirit

I, _____ ,
in the presence of my brothers and sisters in the Lord:
　　　　Wish to commit myself
To being a witness of Christ and of the Father's Love.
However, knowing my weaknesses and my fears,
I confidently offer myself to You
　　　So that You might fill me
　　　With Your strength and Your power,
In order that I might have the courage to announce the Gospel
In Words and in Actions, always and everywhere.

　　　　Bring about in me
A New Pentecost like the one of old, which
In the Upper Room in Jerusalem,
Transformed the disciples into apostles and
Where, in prayer with Mary,
The Mother of Jesus and of the newborn Church,
They awaited Your coming
Which inaugurated the first Evangelization.

　　　　Reveal to me
The secret of union with Mary, so that
With Her I may be totally receptive to
This personal Pentecostal outpouring and
That with her I can stand
At the foot of the Cross
And accept with love the redemptive suffering
Which is at the heart of every apostolate.

Grant that I may
Be stimulated by the Word of God
Which the Church offers in its liturgy each day,
Nourished as often as possible by the Eucharist, and
Partaking regularly in the Sacrament of Spiritual Healing.

Awake in me
A lively faith which will activate my prayer-life,
      By making me available to serve others with love,
And by giving me the words of Your wisdom, so that
In my family, professional and social life,
I may announce with courage and perseverance the truth
That Jesus Christ is Lord.

Give me
A firm and unshakable faith
Which will inspire me to undertake and accomplishIn a faithful
way a resolute and regular apostolate.
A faith which is like a torch in my hands
To fill with light a world which through sin is enveloped in
darkness.

Grant that I may
Share a common bond with the members of my Evangelical cell
Meeting regularly with them to develop and
Deepen our spiritual and apostolic lives, so as to
Encourage one another to perform actions which will advance
God's reign and promote charity and service among all people.

Teach me
To live in trusting union
With the pastors of the Church:
With the Holy Father, the Bishops and the Priests
So that with them I might
Take upon myself my share of responsibility
In the New Evangelization.

Teach me
To live here on earth with renewed Faith
In communion with the glorious Church in Heaven:
Together with the Angels who surround and protect us,
The Saints who inspire and encourage us,
Our deceased who are nearer to us than ever,
And that, having accomplished my mission, my life might end
In the joy and glory of the Most Holy Trinity. Amen.

Saint Joseph, Protector of the Holy Family
Protect me.
Saint Michael the Archangel, from the Powers of Evil,
Protect me.
All the Angels and Saints
Pray for me.

In the name of the Father and of the Son and of the Holy Spirit,
Amen.

Done on _____

Place _____

Signature _____

Father, I am weak and far from virtuous,
help me to realize that you use the weak things
of this world to confound the strong.
Show me how to take the next step in my desire
to build up Your Kingdom.
Bless my humble efforts
so that I may glorify Your name with my life.

(From A.T., Toledo, OH)

I have always been a shy person, and I've never really been able to speak to people on my own initiative about anything, much less religion. But I think I pleased the Lord recently when I spoke about God to one of my daughter's friends. She was having serious problems, and I went to her to invite her to talk. Eventually I asked her if she ever prayed. She said she did, but not much. We had a good talk about God's loving presence and before we were through she had decided to get back to Church. And this eventually led to an entire change in her lifestyle.

Talking to her wasn't a big thing at all. It just happened naturally. I know I can do it with others, and I have. Now I just quietly wait until the Lord lets me know when to speak up. When they tell me their worries, I simply ask, "Have you prayed about it?" I know it pleases God when I do, because it leads to such interesting conversations.

CHAPTER THIRTEEN

Be Confident

The resurrection of Jesus Christ offers us the astounding promise of eternal life. This knowledge gradually awakens an inner confidence that enables us to deal with the problems of life and to pray with heartfelt conviction, *Keep me safe, O God, for You are my hope* (Ps 16:1).

Those who hope in the Lord do more than expect His intervention in times of trouble. They abide with Him at all times. And in doing so they become ever more aware of His loving protection. The smile of God is upon them and they know it. This knowledge supplies a constant source of inner strength.

Our sense of well-being can be jarred by sudden reversals: health problems, accidents, wars, earthquakes. All kinds of things can shock us and disturb our peace, but the virtue of hope stays alive through it all, preserving the soul's untrembling center. In spite of any emotional discomfort we may be feeling at the moment, hope keeps our confidence alive.

One of the strongest incentives to hope is the belief that God is actively involved in our lives. *In Him we live and breathe and have our being* (Ac 17:28).

Hope enables us to live as though we were the children of a King, and God's love becomes so real that we no longer question it. We simply accept it as a wonderful fact of life.

Hope, as described above, is a supernatural virtue because it is oriented directly toward God and the things of God.

Hope, of course, isn't always supernatural. Although very few things happen in life that do not have a spiritual dimension, there are many examples of natural hope where a person has first-rate enthusiasm for some worthy project. Such enthusiasm can lift one to extraordinary heights of performance and courage. Here's an example:

Canadian born Terry Fox of Port Coquitlam, British Columbia, was 22 when he undertook a strenuous trans-Canadian "Marathon of Hope" to raise funds for cancer research. What made his run so special was that in 1977 it was discovered he had a rare form of bone cancer, and most of one leg had to be amputated. While recovering he got the idea for a marathon run across Canada to raise money for cancer research. After months of training, he began his run on April 12, 1980 and ended it on September 1, 1980 in Thunder Bay, Ontario. At first, his story was given a few lines on the back pages of the Canadian newspapers, but by the time he had completed his feat, he had inspired millions of people all over the world, helping to raise $24.7 million.

He was a dying man, yet he found the strength to reach an important goal. He found a way to overcome self-pity and make his last year on earth a meaningful and exciting adventure. He was alive with hope.

Terry Fox died a national hero on June 28, 1981.

The dictionary tells us that hope is an expectation of something desired. Dante went so far as to define it as "a waiting with certitude." It is, therefore, more than wishing. Hope is the confident anticipation of something yet to come.

Jesus said, *I solemnly assure you, the man who hears My words and has faith in Him who sent Me possesses eternal life* (Jn 5:24). Supernatural hope is a gift that empowers us to have confidence in the words and promises of Jesus.

If we look only at ourselves, with our own limitations and sins, we quickly give way to sadness and discouragement. But if we keep our eyes fixed on the Lord, then our hearts are filled with hope. . . . We cannot live without hope. We have to have some purpose in life, some meaning to our existence. We have to aspire to something. Without hope we begin to die (Message of Pope John Paul II to the Youth in America, Los Angeles, CA, Sept. 15, 1987).

The word "virtue" is from the Latin, meaning "power." The theological virtue of hope is an inner power which flows from our faith, giving us *the confident assurance that what we hope for will come to pass* (Heb 11:1).

Since this is a gift of God, it is important to pray for an increase of faith, hope and charity. Christ encouraged us with these words: *Ask and it shall be given to you* (Mt 7:7). The effects of this inner confidence are manifold: we become happier, more energetic, and we grow closer to God. When this awareness is amplified by the realization that God delights in our humble efforts to love Him, we begin to experience a joy this world can never give.

Let's examine some of the immediate fruits of supernatural hope.

The Fruits of Hope

Hope looks for the good in people, instead of
  harping on the worst.
Hope discovers what can be done, instead of
  grumbling about what cannot.
Hope lights candles instead of cursing the darkness.
Hope pushes ahead when it might be easy to quit.
Hope opens doors where despair closes them.
Hope carries on in spite of heartaches.
Hope accepts tragedy with courage.
(Father James Keller, M.M.)

Hope looks for the good in people.

A teacher in Michigan, faced with the discouragement often encountered in today's classrooms writes: "Many people have told me that I would be wasting my time teaching, and that these kids will continue to be just as wild, disobedient and disrespectful as before. However, I thought that, with the grace of God, maybe I could reach them and persuade them to use their tremendous potential."

He succeeded in reaching many of them.

Like this teacher, each one of us has been given a particular mission in life. That mission is itself a gift that will shape our own happiness and the happiness of others. God is ready to provide the strength, courage and vision we need so much, and He is delighted when we ask for His help. That, in part, may be why we derive such happiness ourselves from following our calling.

People animated by divine faith tend to think, pray, and work more effectively. They know they are co-workers with the Lord in making this a better world by helping to build up His Kingdom.

We can begin building the heavenly Kingdom here and now by making this a better world. If we do, fewer people will have cause to be outraged by injustice, and more will have reason to give thanks to God for the gift of life. That, in turn, translates into a happier life for everyone and, in terms of eternity, more souls saved. *They who hope in the Lord will renew their strength* (Is 40:31).

Hope discovers what can be done.

Where there's a will, there's a way. All we have to do is ask for God's help and He will give it.

When Marie Balter was named "Wonder Woman of the Year," she was ecstatic, and a little overwhelmed. After all, she had spent 20 years in various mental institutions, having been diagnosed as a psychotic. Her struggle against the devastating stigma of mental illness was a stunning example of courage and hope. Marie never gave up. After a tormented childhood, she was passed from one foster home to another, and eventually was hospitalized for depression. Things then went from bad to worse.

After years of therapy and fervent prayer, putting her trust in Christ, she managed to persevere in her dream to be a healthy, productive human being. She persevered in her desire and was eventually released and allowed to continue her education. She went on to earn a Master's degree from Harvard University.

Today Marie Balter enjoys a distinguished career as an administrator in the mental health field. Her dream came true. Hope triumphed over adversity. *Praised be the God and Father of our Lord Jesus Christ, He who in His great mercy gave us new birth; a birth unto hope which draws its life from the resurrection of Jesus Christ* (1 P 1:3).

Hope lights candles instead of cursing the darkness.
There are many ways to overcome darkness. One of them is by being a light for others.

J. Copeland Gray lost his sight at the age of 60. Instead of brooding over his plight, he began visiting a veterans' hospital in Buffalo to give encouragement to lonely G.I. patients. Despite his handicap, he wanted to help recovering servicemen find a positive way to channel their energies.

This very act of seeing himself as a healer, instead of a victim, was the breakthrough he needed. His good example was all the veterans needed. He taught them to start becoming healers themselves. "You help yourself when you reach out to help others," he said. "I know I've done a good job when they ask me to come again."

Let your light shine (Mt 5:16).

Hope opens doors where despair closes them.

Little acts of kindness done out of love for God delight Him. Through them, we awaken life-giving hope in others. The Lord uses each one of us in ways we never imagine. Here's a case where a priest touched someone's life without even realizing it.

As a young singer in the 1940's and 50's, Betty Hutton lit up the stage and screen in her pursuit of fame and fortune. The applause of the crowd meant approval and love, two things she desperately needed. Raised by her mother in an atmosphere of promiscuity and alcohol abuse, she lacked the skills and maturity needed to deal cautiously and wisely with Hollywood's fast-talkers. They used her, and then tossed her aside like a squeezed lemon.

Her career plummeted and her hopes were dashed. Unable to cope, she turned to pills and eventually ended up in a detox hospital. A dark cloud enveloped her. Over a period of ten desperate years, she lived in six different mental institutions. She reached the point where she thought she would never be happy again.

Then one day, almost miraculously, an amazing thing happened. While huddled in the corner of a crowded hospital ward, she noticed at the other end of the room a visiting Catholic priest talking to one of the women patients. His kindness so intrigued her that she made a point of speaking to him. On his next visit, Betty asked for his help. The priest had no idea who she was, but he agreed to help her find employment as soon as she was strong enough to be released. That little spark of encouragement made all the difference.

Years later, she said it was that priest's kindness that inspired her to start the long journey back to health. Today she is living a happy and productive life in Rhode Island, assisting young drug abusers to reclaim their sanity and their health. *In the world you will have trouble, but be brave. I have overcome the world* (Jn 16:33).

Hope pushes ahead when it might be easy to quit.

Jesus, speaking for his heavenly Father, made it quite clear that God takes personally the loving service we offer to those in need: *What you did for the least of My brethren, you did for Me* (Mt 25:40).

Because 84 people donated an hour a day every day for two years, a little girl progressed from hopelessness to happiness.

At nine months of age, the Fairlawn, NJ infant was considered irreversibly brain damaged. Surgery had left her with no muscle or eye coordination. Then a dedicated group of housewives, husbands, teenagers and retirees began patterning exercises to re-program the little girl's damaged brain. After one year, the youngster was able to kneel, crawl, and creep. After two years, she could stand and talk.

"We hoped she'd get where she is now," said the child's grateful mother, "but we knew it would be a long shot. God bless everyone who helped us."

God does bless those who help their neighbor. His blessing is itself an expression of His appreciation and pleasure. *Be brave and steadfast and have no fear* (Dt 31:6).

Hope carries on in spite of heartaches.

All stories do not have a happy ending, yet the flame of hope keeps joy alive in the human heart.

One October day in 1946, while Catherine de Vinck was pregnant with her second child, she was overcome by gas leaking from a stove. Her husband José saved her just in time. Six months later, on April 20, 1947, Oliver was born, a beautiful and healthy looking baby boy, but there was something wrong with him.

The parents had their worst suspicions confirmed at Mt. Sinai Hospital in New York City. Oliver was blind and severely brain damaged. The gas his mother had inhaled had reached him causing this severe, incurable condition. The doctors recommended that he be put in an institution.

"He's our son," the parents answered. "We'll take him home, of course."

Oliver was a helpless infant all his life. He never spoke or gave evidence of recognizing anyone. He weighed about 100 pounds most of his adult life. Though he was always immobile and flat on his back, he received such tender care that when he died on March 12, 1980 at the age of 33, he had no bed sores.

His mother said, "Medically speaking, Oliver was always a hopeless case, yet he was such a precious gift for the whole family. He had no apparent usefulness or meaning, and the 'world' would have rejected him as an unproductive burden. But he was a holy innocent, a child of light. Through Oliver, I learned the deepest meaning of compassion." Jesus tells us, *If you live according to My teachings, you will know the truth and the truth will set you free* (Jn 8:31-32).

Hope accepts tragedy with courage.

The late Martin Luther King, Sr., a Baptist preacher from Birmingham, Alabama, managed to survive tragedy and continue his work for the Lord. Not only did he lose his son Martin to an assassin's bullet, but his wife was murdered in an Atlanta church.

While speaking before a large audience years later, he said, "Don't magnify what someone else may be doing and minimize the wrongs on your own part." He stressed the idea that we should be concerned about reaching out to those in need. "The business of the church," he insisted, "is to give everyone a sense of belonging."

Martin Luther King, Sr., forgave his enemies. This was

possible only because his hope was not in this world, but in God. He believed in the coming of the Kingdom, where every tear will be wiped away and every broken fence will be mended. *You will forget your misery; you will remember it as waters that have passed away* (Jb 11:16).

How To Grow in the Virtue of Hope

1. Pray for deliverance from the bonds of sin. You can't be hopeful when you are willingly entangled in evil. *Our battle is not against human forces but against the principalities and powers, the rulers of the world of darkness* (Ep 6:12).

2. Open your heart to Jesus Christ. He is the hope of the world. Let Him be your strength and your joy.

3. Receive the sacraments of the Church. There are special graces in each one, particularly in the Sacrament of Reconciliation where inner healing takes place, and in the Eucharist where the Risen Lord nourishes us with His wisdom and love.

4. Know your purpose. It's vital for you to have a clear idea about your mission in life. God made you for a reason. You have a job to do that nobody else can do. This is the meaning of your existence.

5. Find ways to love your neighbor. You are an individual, it's true. But you are also part of the larger community. God did not call you to live in isolation. You are part of God's people on pilgrimage. Share your gifts with others.

6. Persevere in your good intentions. It is always easy to quit, but as Vince Lombardi, the legendary football coach, once said, "A quitter never wins and a winner never quits." The real goal before you is the development of your Christian character. When you have an unwavering faith and hope, God's strength becomes your strength.

7. Keep your chin up. St. Francis de Sales used to say, "Never be discouraged because you're discouraged." Discouragement will come and go in your life. Don't make too much of it. Lift up your heart and have a new confidence. God's plan for you is an eternity of happiness. *Seek first the Kingdom of God and all things shall be added to you besides* (Mt 6:33).

> There are days when the burdens we carry
> chafe our shoulders and wear us down,
> when the road seems dreary and endless,
> the skies grey and threatening;
> when our lives have no music in them
> and our hearts are lonely,
> and our souls have lost their courage.
> Flood the path with light,
> we beseech Thee, O Lord,
> Turn our eyes
> to where the heavens are full of promise!
>
> *(St. Augustine)*

(From Claire Schutz, Wayne, NJ)

God has always spoiled me . . . it's amazing to know that I am the apple of His eye. I have never done anything special except love Him very much. In return He has given me love, protection, support and a life filled with beauty and wonder.

The world would not accept some of my experiences as evidence of God's love. They would call them crosses. I disagree with the world. I call them love pats from God to keep me close to Him. My leukemia, two diabetic children, widowhood, seven beautiful children, enough food on the table, a beautiful sunset, a glorious sunrise, a quiet moment, a delicate flower, a friend — all these things tell me that God is my Father and He loves me.

CONCLUSION

In the bright and beautiful promise of
eternal happiness, I send you
my warmest deepest sentiments of love.
May you feel the power of God's love
working miracles in your life.
May the Risen Lord help you to remain
strong and unwavering in your faith,
and may He give you a heart full
of love for God and neighbor.
May the Lord be your strength and your joy.

Father John Catoir